GLOBAL
ECONOMIC
TURMOIL
AND THE PUBLIC GOOD

GLOBAL ECONOMIC TURMOIL
AND THE PUBLIC GOOD

Steven Rosefielde
University of North Carolina, USA

Daniel Quinn Mills
Harvard Business School, USA

 World Scientific

NEW JERSEY · LONDON · SINGAPORE · BEIJING · SHANGHAI · HONG KONG · TAIPEI · CHENNAI

Published by

World Scientific Publishing Co. Pte. Ltd.

5 Toh Tuck Link, Singapore 596224

USA office: 27 Warren Street, Suite 401-402, Hackensack, NJ 07601

UK office: 57 Shelton Street, Covent Garden, London WC2H 9HE

Library of Congress Cataloging-in-Publication Data
Rosefielde, Steven.
    Global economic turmoil and the public good / by Steven Rosefielde (University of North Carolina, USA) & D. Quinn Mills (Harvard Business School, USA).
        pages cm
    Includes bibliographical references.
    ISBN 978-9814590501
    1. Global Financial Crisis, 2008–2009. 2. Economic policy. 3. Economic development.
4. Finance, Public. I. Mills, Daniel Quinn. II. Title.
    HB37172008 .R67 2015
    330.9'0511--dc23

                                                                2014037409

British Library Cataloguing-in-Publication Data
A catalogue record for this book is available from the British Library.

In-house Editors: Dipasri Sardar/Philly Lim

Typeset by Stallion Press
Email: enquiries@stallionpress.com

Printed in Singapore

For David Rosefielde

Table of Contents

Executive Summary

The promise of global economic liberalization has given way to a crisis-prone, economically stagnant, politically fragile new world order. The origins of the problems of economic crisis, stagnation, ballooning inequality, middle class affliction and global polarization lie in the political system — they are not primarily economic. It follows that the route to avoiding future financial crises and to restoring economic growth lies in preventing politicians from riding roughshod over prudent economic policy.

The challenge posed by secular stagnation, crises, decay and discord today cannot be adequately understood in traditional terms. The main driver is insider globalization; that is, the worldwide quest by national establishments and their various allies to maximize rewards for themselves derived from government programs, corruption, self-serving regulation, over-taxation, fiscal leverage, credit expansion, liberalization, supra-nationalization and emergent world government.

Globalization on western terms is dead. Russia, China and various nations of the Middle East have been afforded a major opportunity to bend the global power balance their way with multiple instruments including military force, flouting the START arm control agreement, subversion, intimidation, market power and "enlightened conservative" authoritarian ideologies. The resulting struggle for hegemony will exacerbate the gathering economic storm.

There are no easy fixes to the increasing turmoil into which the world is falling because the advocacy of the public good by entrenched politicians and government administrators is hypocritical. Miracles should not be expected. Nonetheless, a different and more effective path is available if democratic publics begin to appreciate the present danger. The people can take direct action to reclaim their sovereignty. They can devise strategies for constraining the rapacity of insiders, including those set forward in this book, and clip the wings of their "public servants".

Preface*

This volume develops, expands and synthesizes themes previously addressed by the authors in *Master of Illusion* (Cambridge University Press, 2007), *Prevention and Crisis Management* (World Scientific, 2012), *Democracy and its Elected Enemies* (Cambridge University Press, 2013), and *Inclusive Economic Theory* (World Scientific, 2014). It stresses the adverse role of state actors in economic and international affairs as is often done in political science, but does so more rigorously with the aid of inclusive economic theory.

The integration of market and government within a unified framework makes it plain that governments today are the primary source of mounting global economic turmoil, not the solution as officials tirelessly claim.

---

*Our view is gradually becoming main stream. See Fukuyama, Francis (2014), "America in Decay: The Sources of Political Dysfunction," *Foreign Affairs*, September/October. Available at http://www.foreignaffairs.com/articles/141729/francis-fukuyama/america-in-decay. Cf. *Economic Conditions Snapshot, September 2014: McKinsey Global Survey results*, September 2014. Available at http://www.mckinsey.com/Insights/Economic_Studies/Economic_Conditions_Snapshot_September_2014_McKinsey_Global_Survey_results?cid=other-eml-alt-mip-mck-oth-1409: "After identifying geopolitical instability as a top risk to global growth for three successive surveys, executives now also cite it most often as a threat to both near- and long-term growth in their own economies. In fact, since we first asked about geopolitical risk, the threat it poses to economic growth has hit record levels in McKinsey's newest survey on economic conditions."

Economics as Alexander Rosenberg correctly argues is not a comprehensively testable science.[1] Data are often unreliable and dis-informative. Theories are fuzzy, and cannot be repeatedly verified under laboratory conditions. Propaganda often compels analysts to operate in a "wilderness of mirrors".[2] Inclusive economic theory does not obviate these deficiencies. However, by integrating neoclassical and neo-realist theories, it provides a superior tool for discerning what Karl Popper calls "truthlike verisimilitude".[3] The method is an advanced form of Popper's "critical rationality", and is vastly more powerful than rival contemporary economic methodologies.

Combining inclusive economics with political science we are able to lucidly describe the increasing disruption of the global economy which is occurring today, its causes and potential cures.

In this book we make predictions. In earlier books we have made predictions also. We are generally right. Many commentators and pundits make predictions that are wrong. This is because those people are generally engaged in wishful thinking — they insist that people, corporations and nations are better than they really are. Their predictions are exercises in romantic illusions. Such predictions do not come true. In contrast, we are neorealists. We do not expect the world to be better than it shows itself to be. Hence, our predictions are most often correct.

---

[1] Rosenberg, Alexander (1994), *Mathematic Politics or Science of Diminishing Returns*, Chicago: University of Chicago Press. "None of our models of science really fit economics at all".

[2] Martin, David (2003), *Wilderness of Mirrors: Intrigue, Deception and the Secrets That Destroyed Two of the Cold War's Most Important Agents*, New York: Lyons Press.

[3] Popper, Karl (1985), *The Open Society and Its Enemies*, New York: Harper & Row. Popper, Karl (1985), "The Rationality Principle", in David Miller, ed., *Popper Selections*, Princeton: Princeton University Press.

Foreword

Commentators and social scientists have broken up our times into parts; they have not tried to fit the parts together; so that our task is substantial. Combining domestic politics, economics and international relations into one coherent story is critical to a full understanding of our future. We have made the attempt.

Acknowledgments

The scope of Global Economic Turmoil and the Public Good is too large to permit us to thank all those who have contributed to its development, but special thanks is due to Wenting Ma for her invaluable research assistance. Susan Rosefielde gave her unstinting support.

Steven S. Rosefielde

Thanks to Jefferson Flanders for many discussions which helped me understand these topics. Thanks also to the Research Division of the Harvard Business School for financial support of research on which this book is partially based.

D. Quinn Mills

Part I
Global Economic Turmoil

Chapter **1**

Playing with Fire

The reader will "have to make up his mind, whether he wants simple answers to his questions, or useful ones — in this as in other economic matters he cannot have both". Joseph A. Schumpeter, Sophus A. Reinert, (interview with Sean Silverthorne), "The Forgotten Book that Helped Shape the Modern Economy", *Working Knowledge*, Harvard Business School, November 7, 2011. http://hbswk.hbs.edu/item/6853.html.

The global economy is becoming increasingly turbulent. Another and more virulent version of the financial crisis is likely, although many vainly hope that if the Federal Reserve can keep interest rates down we will muddle through. Much can be done to prevent another catastrophic financial crisis but probably will not. The key reason for inaction is that political and economic leaders insist that the current economic situation is for the public good. It is not.

The 2008 global financial crisis was supposed to quickstep into a V-shaped recovery and morph thereafter into a protracted period of vibrant global economic growth.[1] The V-shaped recovery did not happen. Instead, seven years after the crisis hit, economic activity in parts of the European Union (EU) remains depressed,[2] post-recovery growth in

[1] "Velocity and the V-shaped Recovery", *Forbes*, October 21, 2008. Retrieved from http://www.forbes.com/2008/10/20/money-recession-recovery-oped-cx_bw_rs_1021wesburystein.html.
[2] "IMF cuts eurozone 2014 growth forecast", July 14, 2014. Retrieved from http://news.yahoo.com/imf-cuts-eurozone-2014-growth-forecast-223727218.html.

America has been anemic, and concern is mounting about a fresh financial crisis.[3] The BRICS (Brazil, Russia, India, China and South Africa) briefly defied economic gravity, but most eventually succumbed to its downward pull.[4] Russia and Brazil crashed, and growth retardation has beset the rest of the miracle club, including China. Brighter days are constantly heralded, but there are sound reasons for skepticism.[5]

These dispiriting results have been brought about by intensifying the excesses which precipitated the 2008 global financial crisis in the first place. Sovereign indebtedness continues to steadily mount,[6] and "bubbling" — creating asset price bubbles via low interest rates and excessive monetary ease — has become the accepted policy elixir for

---

[3] Mirhaydari, Anthony (2014), "Is the Eurozone's Debt Crisis Set to Reignite?" *Money Watch* (July 10). Retrieved from http://www.cbsnews.com/news/is-the-eurozones-debt-crisis-set-to-reignite. "Markets were volatile Thursday, with the Russell 2000 flirting with losses for the year on fresh concerns over the health of the Portuguese banking system". This comes after trading in shares of Portugal's largest bank, Banco Espirito Santo, were halted in the European session after tumbling 19%.

[4] Korhonen, Iikka; Fidrmuc, Jarko and Batorova, Ivana (2012), "Business-cycle Decoupling", in Steven Rosefielde, Masaaki Kuboniwa and Satoshi Mizobata, eds., *Two Asias: The Emerging Postcrisis Divide*, Singapore: World Scientific, pp. 345–358.

[5] Lachman, Desmond (2014), "Seeking Alpha 'The Euro Crisis, Part 2'?" *AEI* (May 21). Retrieved from http://www.aei.org/article/economics/international-economy/the-euro-crisis-part-2/?utm_source=today&utm_medium=paramount&utm_campaign=060414#. U484zySYFWc.email. "Judging by the increasingly upbeat statements of European policy-makers and the currently buoyant market pricing of eurozone sovereign bonds, one could be forgiven for thinking that the euro crisis is now finally behind us. However, to do so would be to ignore a whole slew of underlying economic and political indicators that would suggest a very different story. Those indicators would suggest that at best we are in the phony-war stage of the crisis and that it is only a matter of time before that crisis returns with greater virulence than before. Among the more basic indicators to which the market is paying scant attention is the fact that eurozone public debt levels remain extraordinarily high and are yet to show any clear signs of declining. The public sector sovereign debt to gross domestic product (GDP) level is now as high as 175% in Greece, 133% in Italy, and around 125% in Ireland and Portugal. Making these debt levels all the more troubling is the fact that all of these countries are now showing the clearest signs of austerity fatigue and the lack of political willingness to generate primary budget surpluses of a size sufficient to place those debt ratios on a declining path".

[6] Johnson, Simon and Kwak, James (2012), *White House Burning: The Founding Fathers, National Debt and What it Means to You*, New York NY: Vintage.

accelerating global economic growth. Leaders everywhere are disregarding the handwriting on the wall — economic turmoil ahead — gambling that they personally and their nations will prevail[7]; hoping against hope that there will be stability, prosperity, robust growth and international tranquility in our time.[8] These hopes are going to be dashed for most people, unless there is a swift change of attitude and policy.[9]

How can this be? It has been an axiom of faith for at least a quarter of a millennium that people are "rational"; that reason governs individual and governmental behavior about the problems we face and decisions about how to deal with them. Does not it follow that if wrong decisions are sometimes made, leaders should learn from their mistakes and avoid repeating them? Likewise, should not advances in economic science, information technologies, computerization and management have diminished crisis risk and increased growth potential? Many pundits and politicians tell us that this is the case.

It would be good if their assurances were trustworthy, but the record indicates otherwise. Honest pundits, politicians and social scientists dismiss the dangers ahead because they have broken up our times into parts; they have not tried to fit the parts together. This makes our task substantial. Piecing domestic politics, economics and international relations into one

---

[7] Reinhart, Carmen and Rogoff, Kenneth (2009), *This Time Will be Different: Eight Centuries of Financial Folly*, Princeton NJ: Princeton University Press.

[8] The British Prime Minister (PM) has been hailed as bringing "peace to Europe" after signing a non-aggression pact with Germany. PM Neville Chamberlain arrived back in the United Kingdom (UK) today, holding an agreement signed by Adolf Hitler which stated the German leader's desire never to go to war with Britain again. BBC, September 30, 1938. Retrieved from news.bbc.co.uk/onthisday/hi/dates/stories/september/30/newsid_3115000/3115476.stm.

[9] "Yellen says Fed easy money needed even after recovery: Report", *Reuters*, July 14, 2014. Retrieved from http://finance.yahoo.com/news/yellen-says-fed-easy-money-needed-even-recovery-133651741--business.html. "And so even when the headwinds have diminished to the point where the economy is finally back on track and it's where we want it to be, it's still going to require an unusually accommodative monetary policy", she is quoted as saying in the article that stresses Yellen's role as public servant.

"I come from an intellectual tradition where public policy is important, it can make a positive contribution, it's our social obligation to do this", she says in an online version of the article. "We can help to make the world a better place".

coherent story is critical to a full understanding of our future. *Global Economic Turmoil and the Public Good* fills the gap. It plumbs the paradox of "rational-doublethinking" (fragmented theory and "motivated blindness") to pinpoint what has gone wrong and to clarify why the future is becoming increasingly perilous. It not only describes the danger of a mega global financial crisis looming on the horizon and east–west polarization, but also considers prospects for subsequent decay and social disorder. It documents what has been done since 2008 to forestall financial turbulence and economic sclerosis; analyzes contemporary policies designed to spur accelerated growth, and probes their inadequacies. Most importantly of all, it explains why leaders driven by an indomitable will for personal wealth, privilege and power,[10] persistently do the wrong thing, and it shows how matters can be rectified with the assistance of "inclusive economic theory".[11]

Having Your Cake and Eating It[12]

The mega force driving the globe into economic turmoil is the conviction of political insiders that they can have their cake and eat it too by persistently increasing deficit spending and expanding credit. Once upon a time, it was fashionable to counsel restrained government spending and financial discipline, and to devise adjustment mechanisms to deal with prodigal countries.[13] But times have changed. Government insiders today across the planet have convinced themselves individually and collectively that the best

---

[10] Schopenhauer, Arthur (2010), *The World as Will and Representation*, Cambridge: Cambridge University Press, Vol. 1. Magee, Bryan (1997), *The Philosophy of Schopenhauer*, Oxford: Oxford University Press.

[11] Rosefielde, Steven and Pfouts, Ralph W. (2014), *Inclusive Economic Theory*, Singapore: World Scientific Publishers.

[12] The proverb literally means "you cannot both possess your cake and eat it". An early recording of the phrase is in a letter on March 14, 1538 from Thomas, Duke of Norfolk to Thomas Cromwell, as "a man cannot have his cake and eat his cake". *Letters and Papers, Foreign and Domestic, Henry* VIII, Vol. 13, Part 1, p. 189, Ref. 504.

[13] This was the focus of the absorption approach in international macroeconomic theory. See Haberler, Gottfried von (1976), "The Monetary Approach to the Balance of Payments", *Journal of Economic Literature*, Vol. 14, No. 4, pp. 1324–1328. Obstfeld, Maurice (2001), "International Macroeconomics: Beyond the Mundell–Fleming Model", *IMF Staff Papers*, Vol. 47. Retrieved from https://www.imf.org/external/pubs/ft/staffp/2000/00-00/o.pdf.

course of action for them is to do whatever they please (Schopenhauer's will to power), shifting the adjustment burden willy–nilly on to the shoulders of their victims. They insist that all risks can be managed and whatever is good for them is best for everyone else. The attitude is abetting a new Cold War driven by the complementary delusion that insiders in the conduct of international affairs likewise can have and simultaneously eat their cake,[14] drawing economics and international relations into a common destructive vortex detached from higher reason and ethics.

This book's central thesis is that "having and eating your cake" governments across the globe today led by self-seeking insiders and politicians (politocrats) acting under the cover of various political economic ideals are the principal cause of secular stagnation and inequality, and the growing threats of financial crises, decay, social discord and east–west polarization. Governments are generating these disorders by riding roughshod over the competitive forces of supply and demand, and deflecting blame by pointing fingers everywhere except at themselves. And they are blowing smoke in everyone's eyes by pretending that secular stagnation, inequality, financial crises and international rivalries can be eliminated with more refined neoclassical economic theories, better macroeconomic policies and punitive economic measures (including sanctions imposed on Russia) rather than remedying insider governmental abuses.[15]

Global Economic Turmoil exposes this doublethinking delusion, and details the various ways government practices and policies need to be radically altered to assure global prosperity and tranquility. The book helps readers confront the fact that government insiders and their private sector "partners" improperly acting in their own interests are the primary cause

---

[14] The Monitor's View, "The US–Russia 'great game' over Ukraine", April 1, 2014. Retrieved from http://www.csmonitor.com/Commentary/the-monitors-view/2014/0401/The-US-Russia-great-game-over-Ukraine.

[15] One example of the mentality is reflected in the World Bank's campaign to "share prosperity and mitigate poverty" assuming that government can achieve the goal without significant adverse side effects. See "Shared Prosperity and the Mitigation of Poverty", *World Bank Research Digest*, Vol. 8, No. 2, Winter 2014. Jensen, Donald (2014), "Ukraine Crisis: The US Pushes Back", *Institute of Modern Russia* (April 3). Retrieved from http://imrussia.org/en/russia-and-the-world/704-ukraine-crisis-the-us-pushes-back#.U0Emg16z5w0.email.

of the planet's contemporary economic and geopolitical woes,[16] and that fundamental solutions have to start with downsizing government and disciplining self-seeking insiders.

The danger posed by politicians acting for themselves in association with various interest groups at the people's expense is skillfully camouflaged. In America unofficial spokesmen for the Democrat Party (and Wall Street) like Larry Summers and Paul Krugman purportedly support aggressive money creation, increased deficit spending and national debt to fund egalitarian programs (rather than financial speculators) that they claim are socially progressive, while the Republican Party portrays itself as the advocate of free competition. This makes it appear that the electorate has a clear choice when in fact both parties favor big insider government and assistance to the rich. Both assiduously press for more government stimulus albeit at slightly different levels, each striving to steer funds to its preferred constituents. The dichotomy is not between social democracy and democratic free enterprise. The "welfare" state is taken as given by both sides. The dividing line is between Summers's and Krugman's rhetorical support for aggressive macroeconomic stimulation targeted toward "deserving minorities" (anti-austerity policy),[17] and the Republican Party's preference for less macroeconomic stimulation coupled with Laffer Curve-style business tax incentives and deregulation,[18] and a slightly lower tolerance for excessive national debt. This clash of caricature philosophies dominates most of the media's attention, diverting public scrutiny from the important truth that over-regulation, excess stimulation

---

[16] Former KGB head and Russian PM under Boris Yeltsin, Evgeny Primakov advocates Putin increasing the role of command in Russia's economy and curtailment of the market and justifies the advocacy by pointing to developments in America. "Meanwhile, the US and EU countries increased the influence of the state on the economy during the downturn, and this trend is still continuing today". Primakov, Yevgeny (2014), "Russia's Problems: Why Neoliberal Policy is Unacceptable Today", (January 27). Retrieved from http://valdaiclub. com/economy/66385.html#sendToFriendBox.

[17] Weichenrieder, Alfons (2014), "Many European countries feel haunted by 'excess austerity,'" *SAFE Newsletter Research & Policy Q1*. Retrieved from http://scnem.com/a.php?sid=5s69i.j0k n4d,f=5,u=e1c384d46575b8202accb4e4dfa767e7,n=5s69i.j0kn4d,p=1,artref=3870407.

[18] Laffer, Arthur (2004), "The Laffer Curve: Past, Present, and Future", *Heritage Foundation* (June 1). Retrieved from http://www.heritage.org/research/reports/2004/06/the-laffer-curve-past-present-and-future.

and international adventurism indulged in by both political parties are the roots of America's and by extension the globe's economic turmoil.

What This Book Does Not Say

- There is no role for government.
  Government has three purposes. It should make and enforce just laws in the spirit of the Enlightenment that protect individuals in their honest utility seeking from criminals. It should act as the people's agent in providing prudent compassionate social transfers, and it should protect everyone from the ravages of excess credit creation, leveraging and flimflam speculation.
- Democracy causes underperformance of national economies or of the world economy.
  Democracies which support competitive business environments and avoid excessive regulations, excessive government spending and borrowing can have rapidly expanding economies. Contemporary elected regimes are malperforming not because representative government is intrinsically inferior, but because inferior representatives are putting their private interests ahead of their public duty.
- Globalism causes economic decay.
  Russian sources now argue that globalism ("capitalist internationalism") causes economic decay.[19] We see no evidence of this. Globalism has been and can be again an engine of world economic growth and technological advance, if insiders can be prevented from hijacking it for anti-competitive ends.

We offer evidence in this book that globalism based on liberal principles (business competition, free enterprise, restrained deficit spending, responsible credit creation and limited government) can facilitate global economic growth until gains from technology transfer are exhausted, if insiders refrain from international adventurism. The risks of economic crises and armed conflict can be greatly reduced.

---

[19] http://valdaiclub.com/russia_and_the_world/66605html.

Chapter **2**

Ignoring Today's Dangers

Leaders and investors everywhere today are disregarding economic and political storm warning. They delude themselves into believing that pre-crisis stability, prosperity and robust growth of the early years of the new millennium will be easily restored in our time because anti-crisis safeguards installed after 2008 will prevent another damaging financial crisis. Policy-makers are trying to create good times for everyone relying primarily on monetary expansion, intensified government deficit spending, statutory wage increases and egalitarian transfers. There are debates, but disagreement is narrowly restricted to disputes over the right mix of steroids and entitlements.[1] No serious consideration is being given by politicians and macroeconomic theorists to the long term

---

[1] Moody, Chris, "Why Republicans are Going on Offense about Poverty", *Yahoo News*. Moody reports that the Democrats are preparing a renewed anti-poverty campaign for the Fall elections. The goal is to sharply expand past efforts. The Republicans intend to embrace the same goal, but offer alternative programs. Strain, Michael (2014), "A Bad Month Ends a Typical Year", *AEI Ideas* (January 10). Retrieved from http://www.aei-ideas.org/2014/01/a-bad-month-ends-a-typical-year/?utm_source=today&utm_medium=paramount&utm_campaign=011014.

Either way, it will be more of the same. Retrieved from http://news.yahoo.com/republicans-poverty-middle-class-211700961.html.

causes of global economic growth retardation and the risks of perpetual fiscal and monetary stimulus.

The conversation assumes that the global economy is fundamentally sound, when it actually needs radical economic restructuring. Global well-being today is jeopardized by new forms of antique political economy that harken back to the monarchies of the 18th century. Our current problem is more than one of faulty policies or defective foresight, as most commentators insist. It stems instead from a reversion to economic patterns which preceded Adam Smith's insights dominated by authorities' will to wealth, privilege and power. Just as 18th century governments ruled in the private interests of the crown and aristocracy, their contemporary electoral successors over regulate, over tax, stifle the productive core, and encourage speculative abuses. These and other similarly motivated actions of today's governments are the principal causes of secular stagnation, and contributing factors to the next financial crisis.[2] They also are apt to cause post-crisis, decay and social discord.[3] The only sure way out of the *cul de sac* of secular stagnation, crises, social decay and populist turmoil is eradicating insider privilege and returning to Smith's formula for promoting the wealth of nations: Freedom for individual initiative, business competition and efficient government.

We know how to do these things; we have done them before. But our governments have been captured by politicians who in league with cronies and allies, have stifled initiative with regulation and taxes, crushed competition with special favors for certain firms, and are damaging the public credit with unreasonable levels of deficits and debt.

---

[2] Many observers today predict another financial crisis soon, but usually place responsibility on Wall Street, missing the key point that the financial community is in league with government insiders and that this collusion is only an aspect of the problem, and not the complete cause. For example, see Hartmann, Thom (2013), *The Crash of 2016: The Plot to Destroy America — and What We Can Do to Stop It*, New York NY: Twelve.

[3] Reinhart, Carmen and Rogoff, Kenneth (2009), *This Time Will be Different: Eight Centuries of Financial Folly*, Princeton NJ: Princeton University Press. "China's Financial Squeeze: The Bill for a Borrowing Binge Starts to Come Due", *Wall Street Journal* (January 8). Local government debt today is $3 trillion, nearly double the 2010 figure. Retrieved from http://online.wsj.com/news/article_email/SB10001424052702303848104579307923177519860-lMyQjAxMTA0MDEwMTExNDEyWj.

Post-Crisis Stagnation: The Illusion of Glad Tidings

No one disputes that the post-crisis recovery phase of the 2008 financial crisis has been disappointing in the west and across the globe, but few have paused to reflect whether stagnation and anemic growth can be fixed with sufficient stimulus, or portend the dawn of a dyspeptic epoch. Instead, we are continuing to tell ourselves that a robust economic recovery followed by sustained rapid growth are just around the corner if governments print money and run high enough budgetary deficits. Continuing weak economic and social performance are acknowledged, but not taken to heart except as a rallying cry for repeating the policies causing the substandard performance in the first place.

Some countries still have not recovered to pre-crisis gross domestic product (GDP) levels, and economic growth elsewhere is *subpar*. Unemployment is abnormally high and labor market participation rates low, compounded by widening income and wealth inequality despite extraordinary government efforts to bolster aggregate effective demand.

These facts are important because they provide a solid foundation for investigating alternative futures. Two possibilities deserve particular attention. The first recently elaborated by Lawrence Summers and Paul Krugman which reflects the dominant mood of "rational-wishful thinking" argues that while America is caught in the vise of secular stagnation, increased deficit spending will save the day.[4] No one it seems is ever expected to pay the piper.

---

[4] Krugman, Paul (2009), *The Return of Depression Economics and the Crisis of 2008*, New York NY: WW Norton Company. Summers, Lawrence (2013), "Washington Must Not Settle for Secular Stagnation", *Financial Times* (December 5). Retrieved from http://www.ft.com/cms/s/2/ba0f1386-7169-11e3-8f92-00144feabdc0.html#ixzz2pi6xfiEe. Pethokoukis, James (2013), "The Slump That New Ends: Does the US Face 'Secular Stagnation'?" *AEI* (November 19). Blodget, Henry (2013), "Has the US Entered a 'Permanent Slump'?" *Daily Ticker* (November 18). Retrieved from http://finance.yahoo.com/blogs/daily-ticker/u-economy-entered-permanent-slump-165120719.html. "Summers speculates that the natural interest rate 'consistent with full employment'" fell "to negative 2% or negative 3% sometime in the middle of the last decade". But conventional monetary policy cannot push rates that low. The dreaded Zero Lower Bound. Thus, Summers concludes, "We may well need, in the years ahead, to think about how we manage an economy in which the zero nominal interest rate is a chronic and systemic inhibitor of economic activity, holding our economies back, below their potential". Greenspan, Alan (2013), "Never Saw it Coming", *Foreign Affairs* (November/December). Retrieved from http://www.foreignaffairs.com/articles/140161/alan-greenspan/

The second future postulates that growth retardation cannot be reversed without radical economic reform, and predicts that excessive macroeconomic stimulation will not only cause another devastating global financial crisis,[5] but will usher in an epoch of global decay and discord. This is the future that we consider most likely.

Today's situation is compellingly illuminated with a series of graphs complied by the Economic Policy Institute (EPI).[6] The story they tell establishes the common ground for investigating whether increased macroeconomic stimulation is sufficient to carry us forward, or whether instead, radical economic reform is needed to forestall another financial crisis.

Figures 2.1–2.5 confirm that the American economy is not providing enough positions for jobseekers, despite shrinking labor force participation (some are discouraged workers who never found jobs in the first place and so are not counted by the EPI.[7] Figure 2.1 indicates that the 2008

---

never-saw-it-coming. Cosgrave, Jenny (2014), "Summers: US faces a 'Downton Abbey' economy", *CNBC* (February 17). Retrieved from http://www.cnbc.com/id/101421153.

[5] John Taylor has dismissed the Summers–Krugman secular stagnation crisis as Hokum because he believes that free markets assure a robust American economic recovery. However, while he is justified in challenging Krugman's liquidity trap framework, his own critique of abusive American government points to a plausible alternative explanation for the United States' economic dyspepsia. See Taylor, John (2014), "Economic Hokum of 'Secular Stagnation': Blaming the Market for the Failure of Bad Government policies is no more persuasive now than it was in the 1930s", *Wall Street Journal* (January 1). Retrieved from http://online.wsj.com/news/article_email/SB10001424052702304858104579263953 449606842-lMyQjAxMTA0MDAwMjEwNDIyWj.

[6] www.stateofworkingamerica.org. The EPI is a Washington DC think tank founded in 1986 by left-liberal economists Jeff Faux, Lester Thurow, Ray Marshall, Barry Bluestone, Robert Reich, and Robert Kuttner. Thurow, for example, is a longtime advocate of a political and economic system of the Japanese and European type, in which governmental involvement in the direction of the economy is far more extensive than is presently the case in the United States — a model that has come to be known as "Third Way". See Thurow, Lester (1980), *Zero Sum Society*, New York NY: Basic Books.

[7] Former Chief Economist to Vice President Joseph Biden, Jr., Jared Bernstein reports that American unemployment counting all missing workers January 2014 is 10.2%. He contends that the official 6.7% instantaneous rate is misleading. See Bernstein, Jared (2014), "The Wrong Guidepost on Unemployment", *Yahoo News* (January 15). Retrieved from http://economix.blogs.nytimes.com/2014/01/15/the-wrong-guidepost-on-unemployment/? partner=yahoofinance.

7.9 million more jobs are needed to dig out of the hole left by the Great Recession

Payroll employment and the number of jobs needed to keep up with the growth in the potential labor force, 2000–2013

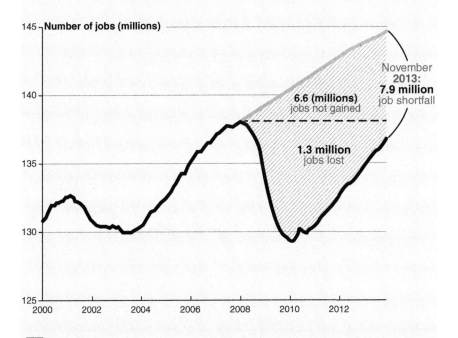

Source: EPI analysis of Bureau of Labor Statistics Current Employment Statistics and estimates of the potential labor force from the Congressional Budget Office *Budget and Economic Outlook: Fiscal Years 2012 to 2022*

This chart originally appeared at: go.epi.org/2013-jobs-gap

ECONOMIC POLICY INSTITUTE

Figure 2.1.   Jobs gap.

financial crisis and its aftermath cost America 7.9 million jobs as of November 2013. The figure for November 2014 is 7.4 million despite the gain of 1.7 million jobs in 2014.[8]

---

[8] In November 2013, the labor market had 1.3 million fewer jobs than when the recession began in December 2007. Further, because the potential labor force grows every month, the economy would have had to add 6.6 million jobs just to preserve the labor market health that

A key barometer of labor market health remains the same today as at recession's end

Employment-to-population ratio of workers age 25–54, 2006–2013

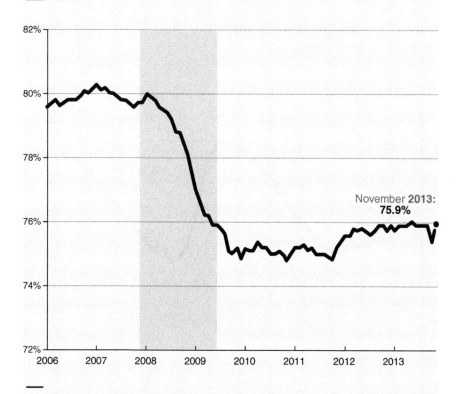

Note: Shaded area denotes recession.

Source: EPI analysis of Current Population Survey public data series

This chart originally appeared at: go.epl.org/2013-epop

ECONOMIC POLICY INSTITUTE

Figure 2.2.   Labor force participation.

prevailed in December 2007. Counting jobs lost plus jobs that should have been gained to absorb potential new labor market entrants, the US economy had a jobs shortfall of 7.9 million in November 2013. The number of potential jobseekers increased 1.3 million using EPI's estimator, while the number of new jobs created was 1.7 million. See http://www.ncsl.org/research/labor-and-employment/national-employment-monthly-update.aspx.

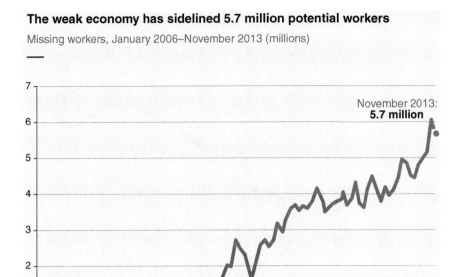

The weak economy has sidelined 5.7 million potential workers

Missing workers, January 2006–November 2013 (millions)

Note: "Missing workers" are potential workers who, due to weak job opportunites, are neither employed nor actively seeking work. Volatility in the number of missing workers in 2006–2008, including cases of negative numbers of missing workers, is the result of month-to-month variability in the sample. The pool of missing workers created by the Great Recession began ti form and grow in late 2008.

Source: EPI analysis of Mitra Toossi, "Labor Force Projections to 2016: More Workera in Their Golden Years," Bureau of Labor Statistics *Monthly Labor Review*, November 2007, http://www.bls.gov/opub/mlr/2007/11/art3full.pdf; and Current Population Survey public data series

This chart originally appeared at: go.epl.org/2013-missing-workers

ECONOMIC POLICY INSTITUTE

Figure 2.3.   Discouraged workers.

The net shrinkage in labor force participation illustrated in Figure 2.2 reveals that the share of 25- to 54-year-olds with a job has barely budged from the 2009 recession trough. If workers who left the labor force because they were discouraged by the 2008 crisis are classified as involuntarily unemployed the unemployment rate would be grimly higher.

Ordinary workers have been due a rise for the last decade

Real average hourly wage growth, by percentile, 2000–2012

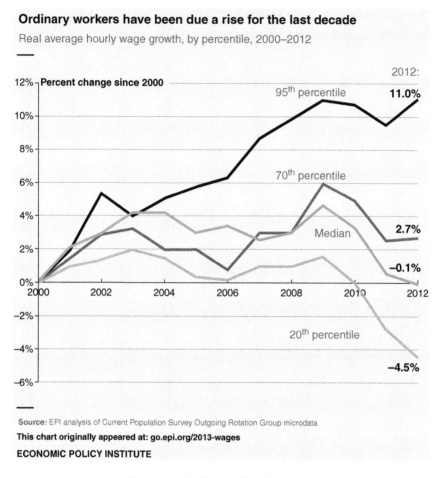

Figure 2.4.   Falling working class wages.

Figure 2.3 provides an estimate of these missing workers.[9] The EPI faults the weak economy for sidelining 5.9 million potential jobseekers.

This weakness cannot be explained in conventional Keynesian macroeconomic terms by resistance to wage cuts ("sticky wages").[10] Figure 2.4

---

[9] Johnson, Rodney (2014), "The Sun Always Shines at the BLS", *Economy & Markets* (June 18).
[10] John Maynard Keynes is the founder of modern macroeconomic theory. He argued that wage and price rigidities prevented economies from adjusting to negative shocks that caused depressions and advocated deficit spending as the antidote. See Keynes,

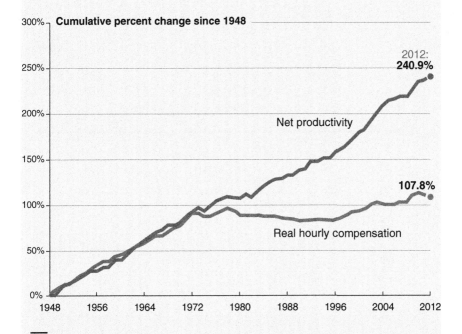

The root of American inequality: wages detaching from productivity

Net productivity and real hourly compensation of production/nonsupervisory workers, 1948–2012

Figure 2.5.   Wage under compensation.

shows that the real inflation adjusted wages of the bottom 70% of American workers have been flat or falling since 2002, in stark contrast to the soaring labor productivity indicated in Figure 2.5. Even though the

John Maynard (1936), *The General Theory of Employment, Interest and Money*, London: Macmillan Cambridge University Press, for Royal Economic Society.

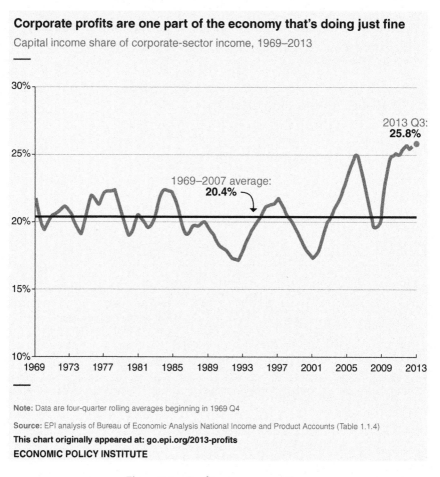

Corporate profits are one part of the economy that's doing just fine

Capital income share of corporate-sector income, 1969–2013

Figure 2.6.   Profit over compensation.

inflation adjusted benefit to employers from hiring workers has steadily increased, demand for labor has plummeted. Neoclassical economic theory teaches that rational employers should hire workers whenever marginal (additional) revenue exceeds marginal cost (there are untapped profits), but this is not happening. Something clearly is amiss. Either the rationality axiom (rational suppliers maximize profits) is wrong, or there are countervailing factors at play.

This deduction is underscored by data on corporate profits and executive compensation. Figure 2.6 demonstrates that corporate profit rates (capital's share of income) in 2013 are at 44 year peak. Executive compensation

The disparity between CEO pay and typical worker wages is climbing back up into the stratosphere

CEO-to-worker compensation ratio, 1965–2012

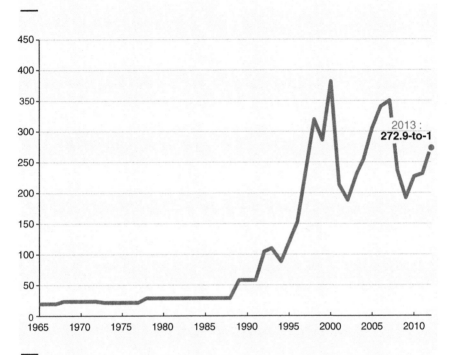

Note: CEO compenstion includes salary, bonuses, restriced stock grants, options exercised, and long-term incentive payments for CEOs at the top 350 firms ranked by sales. The measure of a typical worker's pay is the average annual compensation of a full-time, full-year production/nonsupervisory worker in the firms' major industries.

Source: EPI analysis of Compustat's ExecuComp database, Bureau of Labor Statics Current Employment Statistics, and Bureau of Economic Analysis National Income and Product Accounts

This chart originally appeared at: go.epi.org/2013-ceo-pay
ECONOMIC POLICY INSTITUTE

Figure 2.7.   Wage gap.

has followed suit bolstering long established disparities between executive and worker compensation displayed in Figure 2.7. These trends are apt to persist, other thing equal because wages and salaries of young new market entrants are deteriorating, in part due to the emerging "internship" practices compelling jobseekers to gratuitously work long periods before being treated as regular employees (Figure 2.8). The situation for technical workers is not substantially better (see Figure 2.9).

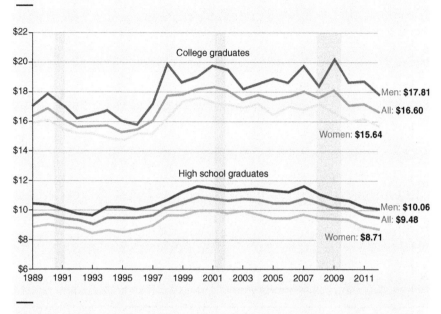

A college degree is no sure ticket to adequate wage growth

Real average hourly wages of young workers, by education, 1989–2012 (2012 dollars)

Note: Data are for college graduates age 21–24 and high school graduates age 17–20 who are not enrolled in further schooling. Shaded areas denote recessions.

Source: EPI analysis of Current Population Survey Outgoing Rotation Group microdata

This chart originally appeared at: go.epi.org/2013-young-workers
ECONOMIC POLICY INSTITUTE

Figure 2.8.   Falling college graduate wages.

The present danger — as the EPI perceives it — therefore is a blighted future of substandard economic growth, stagnation or worse, exacerbated by abnormally high unemployment and underemployment, widening income and wealth disparities between corporate executives and workers (including the middle class), and deteriorating conditions for Black and Hispanic retirees (see Figures 2.10 and 2.11).[11] The framework is gaining

[11] http://news.yahoo.com/why-racial-wealth-gap-could-spell-doom-americas-183454552. html. Global Policy Solutions argues that ignoring our escalating racial wealth disparities will lead to "'national peril'. *Beyond Broke: Why Closing the Racial Wealth Gap is a Priority for National Economic Security*". According to the report, between 2005 and 2011, the median net

Tech credentials are no guarantee that wages rise as the economy expands

Average annual earnings of US employees in semiconductors, software publishing, computer programming, and computer system design, 1994–2010 (2012 dollars)

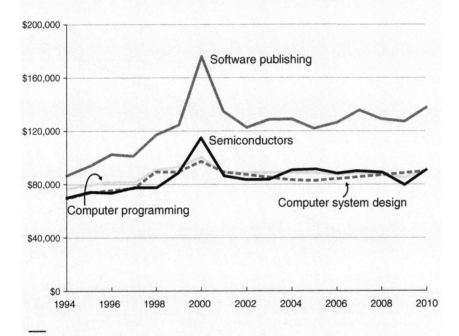

Source: William Lazonick, *Sustainable Property in the New Economy? Business Organisation and High-Tech Employment in the United States,* Upjohn Institute of Employment Research, 2009, updated by Lazonick using U.S. Cenus Bureau County Business Patterns data and provided to EPI

This chart originally appeared at: go.epi.org/2013-tech
ECONOMIC POLICY INSTITUTE

Figure 2.9.   Stagnant tech wages.

worth of minority households remained at recession-era levels, "reflecting a drop of 58% for Latinos, 48% for Asians, [and] 45% for African Americans", compared to just 21% for whites. Moreover, the differences in both net worth and cash on hand are even more striking.

Beyond Broke researchers found the median liquid wealth for Latinos is a mere $340, while African Americans have just $200 in liquid assets. On the other hand, Asians hold $19,500 in median liquid wealth, compared to $23,000 by whites. Furthermore, Blacks and Latinos are twice as likely as whites to have no financial assets".

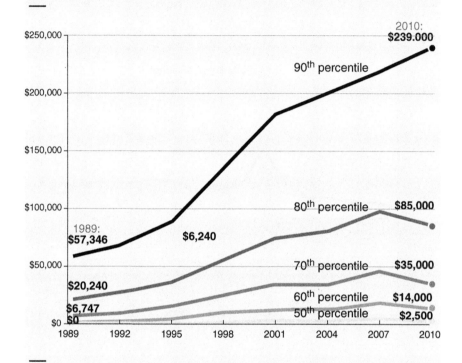

The failed 401(k) revolution has heightened inequality, not provided secure retirement

Savings in retirement accounts of households age 26–79, by percentile, 1989–2010 (2010 dollars)

Figure 2.10.   Declining household savings.

currency across the political spectrum as democrats and republicans tussle over who owns the social justice issue in future elections.[12]

---

[12] Brooks, Arthur (2014), "A Conservative Social Justice Agenda: Time for Conservatives to Champion Struggling Americans *AEI*" (January 31). Retrieved from http://www.aei. org/issues/a-conservative-social-justice-agenda?utm_source=today&utm_medium= paramount&utm_campaign=013114. "The Obama administration's 'progressive' agenda

Retirement inequality hurts minorities

Mean savings in retirement accounts of households age 26–79, by race/ethnicity, 1989–2010 (2010 dollars)

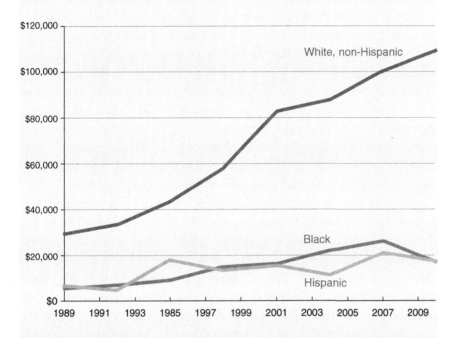

Note: Retirement account savings include savings in 401(k) and other defind-contribution plans, IRAs (including employer-sponsored SEP IRAs and SIMPLE IRAs), and Keogh plans for small businesses. In this figure, "black" and "Hispanic" are not mutually exclusive categories, so a black person of Hispanic origin will be included in both categories.

Source: EPI analysis of Survey of Consumer Finance microdata

This chart originally appeared at: go.epi.org/2013-401k-race-ethnicity

ECONOMIC POLICY INSTITUTE

Figure 2.11. Deficient minority household savings.

---

has left the poor behind. Years after the Great Recession, real need persists. The left's misguided policies and materialistic culture only exacerbate the problem. It is conservatives and libertarians who must be struggling Americans' true champions". "The number of citizens who rely on 'food stamps' has soared by 50% since early 2009; Just 63% of Americans are working or seeking work, the lowest rate since the 1970s; Crisis-level unemployment persists in vulnerable communities — 36% for African–American teens". "Vulnerable people need three things: Personal moral transformation, material relief, and the opportunity to rise".

Although the EPI does not offer a lucid explanation of these trends, it does propose three solutions. First, it suggests discarding austerity (see Figure 2.12), defined as deficit spending below levels needed to restore full employment. Deficit spending has averaged approximately $1.5 trillion annually since 2008 in absolute terms ($500 billion in 2014), which although immense is considered stingy judged as a share of GDP. Second, the EPI recommends nearly doubling the minimum wage to stimulate consumer demand and diminish income inequality (see Figure 2.13). Third, it advises replacing individual retirement accounts with guaranteed state pensions to bolster consumer confidence.[13] The combination EPI claims will increase aggregate effective consumer demand spurring output and employment growth, and will redress the widening gap between labor productivity and wages, without incurring excessive monetary and financial risks — intolerably high inflation, fresh financial crises and microeconomic distortions.

The data provided by the EPI in Figures 2.1–2.13 are convincing. They support Summers's and Krugman's contention that the US is now in a period of "secular stagnation". Even using official statistics, which we consider significantly over-stated, economic growth has been disappointing almost everywhere in the world since 2008. Given the anticipated stimulatory effects of "internal devaluations" (reduced costs of labor, capital and materials), huge government deficit spending (in absolute and relative terms), monetary expansion, cheap money and external currency devaluations; economic growth and the rebound in employment should have been more vigorous.

---

[13] The EPI's Figure 1.9 is misleading. "The US Census Bureau. Data from the Current Population Survey, or CPS, form the basis of the Social Security Administration's Income of the Aged publication series — which is widely cited as showing that Americans' inadequate retirement incomes force them to increasingly rely on Social Security benefits. But the CPS fails to count most of the income Americans derive from 401(k) and IRA plans, as well as significantly understating the percentage of current American workers who are saving for retirement". The CPS ignores 60% of the income that retirees receive. See Schieber, Sylvester and Biggs, Andrew (2014), "Biggs and Schieber: Retirees are not Headed for the Poor House", *Wall Street Journal* (January 23). Retrieved from http://online. wsj.com/news/article_email/SB10001424052702304603704579329012635470796- lMyQjAxMTA0MDIwNDEyNDQyWj. President Obama introduced a new supplementary retirement plan to help invigorate consumer confidence. Yuki Noguchi, "Meet the myRA — Obama's New Retirement Plan", January 29, 2014. Retrieved from http://www.npr.org/ 2014/01/29/268404392/meet-the-myra-obamas-new-retirement-plan.

Austerity (historically low public spending) explains why we're so far from a full recovery

Real government spending in recessions and susequent recoveries

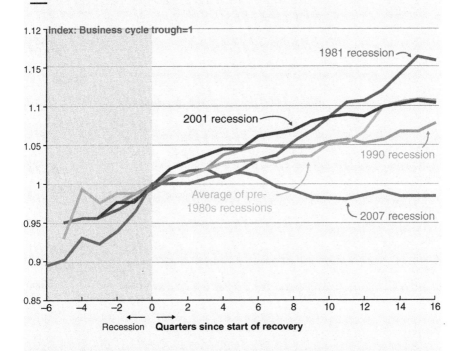

Note: The average of all pre-1980s recessions is the average of government expenditures for the six recessions and subsequent recoveries between 1953 and 1981.

Source: EPI analysis of Bureau of Economic Analysis National Income and Product Accounts (Table 1.1.6)

Updated from the chart That originally appeared at: go.epi.org/2013-austerity

ECONOMIC POLICY INSTITUTE

Figure 2.12.   Recession deficit spending.

The correspondence between the descriptive facts and Summers's and Krugman's story however does not mean that their analysis is complete.[14] Neither their diagnosis (that government spending is inadequate, which they call "austerity") nor their prescriptions (perpetual high deficit

---

[14] Rosefielde, Steven and Pfouts, Ralph W. (2014). *Inclusive Economic Theory*, Singapore: World Scientific.

Restoring the minimum wage will ensure that more of the benefits of rising productivity go to regular workers

Real value of the federal minimum wage, 1968–2013 and 2013–2016 under proposed increase to $10.10 by 2016, compared with its value had it grown at the rate of productivity or average workers wages (2013 dollars)

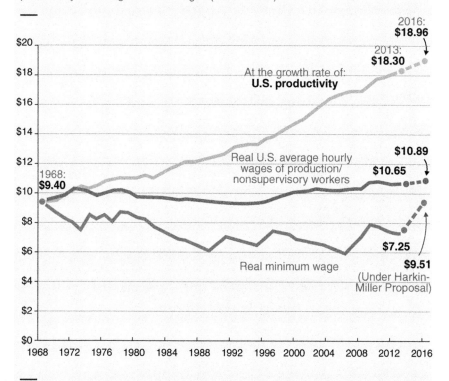

Note: Dollars are deflated using CPI-U-RS and CBO inflation projections. Projected wage values are based on CBO inflation projections, average wage and productivity growth from 2002 to 2006 (the last full regular business cycle), and the proposal to raise the federal minimum wage to $10.10 by 2016.

Source: EPI analysis of Total Economy Productivity Data from the Bureau of Labour Statistics (BLS) Labour Productivity and Costs program, BLS Current Employment Statistics, Current Population Survey Outgoing Rotation Group microdata, the Congressional Budget Office's *Budget and Economic Outlook: Fiscal Years 2013–2023*, and the U.S. Department of Labour Wage and Hour Division's "History of the Federal Minimum Wage", http"//www/dol.gov/whd/minwage/chart.htm

This chart originally appeared at: go.epi.org/2013-min-wage
ECONOMIC POLICY INSTITUTE

Figure 2.13.   Minimum wage trends.

spending, easy money and doubling the minimum wage) are sound.[15] The developed world including the US has been doing what they, the EPI and Obama administration recommend since 2008,[16] and it has made matters worse, not better.[17] Continuing to do more of what they recommend will exacerbate this deterioration.

Political Economy of Secular Stagnation

The hidden assumption of the Summer–Krugman model is that America's miss regulated economic system is superior to democratic free enterprise (unfettered markets with prudent public programs, complemented with ironclad minority property rights protections), even though they recognize that the US economy departs significantly from

---

[15] Summers has moved away from advocating "easy money" and now stresses intensified deficit spending. "The third approach — and the one that holds most promise — is a commitment to raising the level of demand at any given level of interest rates, through policies that restore a situation where reasonable growth and reasonable interest rates can coincide. This means ending the disastrous trend towards ever less government spending and employment each year — and taking advantage of the current period of economic slack to renew and build up our infrastructure. If the government had invested more over the past five years, our debt burden relative to our incomes would be lower: allowing slackening in the economy has hurt its potential in the long run". Summers, Lawrence (2013), "Washington Must Not Settle for Secular Stagnation", *Financial Times* (December 5). Retrieved from http://www.ft.com/cms/s/2/ba0f1386-7169-11e3-8f92-00144feabdc0.html#ixzz2pi6xfiEe.

[16] "Obama's 2014 State of the Union address: Full text", January 28, 2014. Retrieved from http://www.cbsnews.com/news/obamas-2014-state-of-the-union-address-full-text/.

[17] Schwab, Klaus (2014), "The Global Economy 2014", *Project Syndicate* (January 22). Retrieved from digital@project-syndicate.org. Schwab is executive chairman of the World Economic Forum. He writes "The Fed's QE policy, and variants of it elsewhere, have caused the major central banks' balance sheets to expand dramatically (from $5–6 trillion prior to the crisis to almost $20 trillion now), causing financial markets to become addicted to easy money. This has led, in turn, to a global search for yield, artificial asset-price inflation, and misallocation of capital. As a result, the longer QE lasts, the greater the collateral damage to the real economy. The concern now is that when the Fed begins to taper QE and dollar liquidity drains from global markets, structural problems and imbalances will resurface. After all, competitiveness-enhancing reforms in many advanced economies remain far from complete, while the ratio of these countries' total public and private debt to GDP is now 30% higher than before the crisis".

the competitive ideal,[18] and that social transfers are inefficient. More federal governance for them always is beneficial, and accordingly is the cure, not a cause of secular stagnation. More and better government, bigger deficits, higher debts, heavier corporate and middle class taxation, smarter regulation and sterner business discipline are seen as the surest path to "socially responsible" rejuvenation. It does not matter that two generations are saddled with unmanageable education debts,[19] and have set aside little to fund their retirement.[20] Their only caveat is that "demand-side" measures must take pride of place because "supply-side" reforms take too long and could perversely intensify "deflation".[21] The approach cannot

---

[18] The competitive ideal is often called Pareto optimality. For a full analysis of the concept see Rosefielde, Steven and Pfouts, Ralph W. (2014), *Inclusive Economic Theory*, Singapore: World Scientific Publishers. Applied theorists only use the Pareto ideal as a benchmark. They conceive competition as a process among corporate clusters each with its own complex multinational supply chains. This incomplete competition sustains market power. It is inefficient, but better than the alternative. Porter, Michael (1990), *The Competitive Advantage of Nations*, London: Macmillan.

Economists also sometimes use the term "national competitiveness" and frequently recommend government subsidization of research and development and startups to foster the export sector. Paul Krugman considers "national competitiveness" to be potentially anticompetitive because it subsidizes over-exporting. See Krugman, Paul (1994), "Competitiveness: A Dangerous Obsession", *Foreign Affairs* (March/April). Retrieved from http://www.foreignaffairs.com/articles/49684/paul-krugman/competitiveness-a-dangerous-obsession.

[19] http://www.asa.org/policy/resources/stats/. Student debt exceeds one trillion dollars.

[20] There are two aspects to the looming retirement crisis. First, pensions are under-funded to the tune of one trillion dollars, and second private savings needed to supplement social security are at a postwar low. See "The trouble with pensions: Falling short — Workers are sleepwalking towards an impoverished old age", *The Economist*, June 12, 2008. Retrieved from http://www.economist.com/node/11529345. "Harkin Unveils Legislation to Address Retirement Crisis, Rebuild Private Pension System". Harkin, Chair of Senate Pensions Committee, Proposes "Universal, Secure, Adaptable (USA) Retirement Funds Act" to Expand Access to Privately-Run, Portable Retirement Plans", January 30, 2014. Retrieved from http://www.harkin.senate.gov/press/release.cfm?i=349368.

[21] Supply-side fundamentals include "labor force skills, companies' capacity for innovation, structural tax reform and assuring the long-run sustainability of entitlement program". "Indeed, measures that raise supply could have the perverse effect of magnifying

be falsified because it lacks a rigorous theoretical structure. Whatever the government does, and whatever the results, leaders always can claim that their actions were best.

Beyond False Science

Behind the Krugman–Summers recommendations is a misunderstanding of the economy and its dynamics. This false science might be innocuous if the state mostly did the right thing even though its intentions and methods were faulty.[22] But, the facts belie the presumption. Governments do not and cannot optimally plan. They do not know individuals' preferences. They do not know supply possibilities. They do not have their own complete transitive (coherent) preferences. They do not know how their actions affect the well-being of each individual and the community at large.[23]

If they did know individual preferences, they do not have the computational technologies to choose for them, and worse still leaders do not care about social welfare optimization because they have hidden agendas. There is no merit to the claim that the government comprehensively knows best and does the right thing.[24]

None of this means that government cannot serve limited useful purposes.[25] However, it does imply that governments themselves always should be viewed as prime suspects when economic systems become

---

deflationary pressure". Summers, Lawrence (2013), "Washington Must Not Settle for Secular Stagnation", *Financial Times* (December 5). Retrieved from http://www.ft.com/cms/s/2/ba0f1386-7169-11e3-8f92-00144feabdc0.html#ixzz2pi6xfiEe.

[22] Hegel, Georg Wilhelm Friedrich (2001), *The Philosophy of History*, Kitchener, Ontario, Canada: Batoche. Tucker, Robert (1956), "The Cunning of Reason in Hegel and Marx", *The Review of Politics*, Vol. 18, No. 3, pp. 269–295.

[23] Rosefielde, Steven and Pfouts, Ralph W. (2004), *Inclusive Economic Theory*, Singapore: World Scientific, Chapters 2 and 3.

[24] Witness the vanished Soviet Union. Rosefielde, Steven (2007), *Russian Economy From Lenin to Putin*, New York NY: Wiley.

[25] Max Weber laid out the fundamental long ago. See Weber, Max (1978), *Economy and Society*, Berkeley CA: University of California Press.

sclerotic and macroeconomically unstable.[26] The "secular stagnation" that Summers and Krugman perceive in the data is mostly the government's doing. The American government abuses presidential executive orders,[27] miss regulates, excessively mandates, over-taxes, stealthily taxes, abets private sector speculation, miss entitles, miss transfers, incentivizes welfare dependency and feigned disability over employment,[28] and politicizes science and education. These are the principle causes of economic lethargy; not under-consumption,[29] or inequality.[30]

---

[26] Taylor, John (2009), *Getting Off Track: How Government Actions and Interventional Caused, Prolonged, and Worsened the Financial Crisis*, Palo Alto: Hoover Institution Press. Acemoglu, Daron and Robinson, James (2012), *Why Nations Fail: The Origins of Power, Prosperity and Poverty*, New York NY: Crown.

[27] Mason, Jeff (2014), "Obama Signs Order to Raise Minimum Wage for Federal Contractors", *Reuters* (February 12). Retrieved from http://news.yahoo.com/obama-sign-order-federal-minimum-wage-hike-wednesday-110247693--business.html. Obama's action is an usurpation of Congressional authority, and an arbitrary tax on the public because the expense must be funded with taxes or borrowed funds.

[28] Lowrey, Annie (2014), "States Cutting Weeks of Aid to Jobless", *Wall Street Journal* (January 22). Cutting the maximum number of weeks of unemployment has stimulated employment. Cf. Maki, Dennis and Spindler, Z.A. (1975), "The Effect of Unemployment Compensation on the Rate of Unemployment in Great Britain", *Oxford Economic Papers*, New Series, Vol. 27, No. 3, pp. 440–454.

[29] Keynes claimed that aggregate demand is deficient during depressions because unemployed workers cannot afford to consume as much as they did when they were working. This is often referred to under consumptionism. There are pre-Keynesian and Marxist versions of the same basic idea. Cf. Record, Robert (2014), "How the War on Poverty Was Lost: Fifty years and $20 trillion later, LBJ's goal to help the poor become self-supporting has failed", *Wall Street Journal* (January 7). Retrieved from http://online.wsj.com/news/article_email/SB10001424052702303345104579282760272285556-lMyQjAx MTA0MDAwODEwNDgyWj. Cf. Leightner, Jonathan (2014), *The Limits of Monetary, Fiscal, and Trade Policies: International Comparisons and a Solution*, Singapore: World Scientific Publishers.

[30] Piketty, Thomas (2014), *Capital in the Twenty-First Century*, Cambridge MA: Harvard University Press. Piketty recommends a global wealth tax to redress the planet's economic woes. Cf. Worstall, Tim (2014), "Why Thomas Piketty's Global Wealth Tax Won't Work", *Forbes* (March 30). Retrieved from http://www.forbes.com/sites/timworstall/2014/03/30/why-thomas-pikettys-global-wealth-tax-wont-work/. "The Super Rich Are Richer Than We Thought, Hiding Huge Sums, New Reports Find", *Huff Post*, (April 12, 2014). Retrieved from http://www.huffingtonpost.com/2014/04/12/super-rich-richer_n_5138753.html?

Likewise, perpetually mounting excessive public indebtedness, imprudent insurance guarantees (examples include subprime mortgage loans and now Obama's Affordable Care Act),[31] excessive credit creation and printing money, the promotion of excessively risky financial instruments (derivatives), and pro-speculative financial miss regulation are basic causes of macroeconomic disorders such as mega-financial crises, not proofs of responsible economic management.[32]

---

utm_hp_ref=email_share. Piketty is in the process of becoming canonized by political forces pushing for egalitarianism. See "Capital Man", *Chronicle of Higher Education*, April 17, 2014. "Thomas Piketty is economics' biggest sensation. He's also the field's fiercest critic". "On Monday, Piketty's stops included the White House Council of Economic Advisers, the Government Accountability Office, and the office of the Treasury secretary, Jacob Lew, who summoned him for a private sit-down to discuss his proposal for a progressive tax on wealth. On Tuesday, he appeared in the company of Nobelists: George Akerlof, who, introducing Piketty to a group at the International Monetary Fund, declared that he had 'entered rock stardom — economist-style'; and Robert Solow, who, at the EPI, where a crowd of several hundred had braved a freezing downpour to hear Piketty talk, praised the originality of his argument and the 'sheer collection, presentation, and analysis' of his data, predicting that "we're going to be digesting that for a long time". Saez, Emmanuel and Zucman, Gabriel (2014), "The Distribution of US Wealth, Capital Income and Returns since 1913". Retrieved from http://gabriel-zucman.eu/files/SaezZucman2014Slides.pdf. Zucman, Gabriel (2013), "The Missing Wealth of Nations: Are Europe and the US Net Debtors or Net Creditors?," *Quarterly Journal of Economics*, Vol. 128, No. 3, pp. 1321–1364. "8% of the global financial wealth of households is held in tax havens, three-quarters of which goes unrecorded". Some carry Piketty's claim further contending that rapid growth necessitates egalitarianism. See Hoeller, Peter; Joumard, Isabelle and Koske, Isabell (2014), "Reducing Income Inequality While Boosting Economic Growth: Can it be Done? Evidence from OECD Countries", *The Singapore Economic Review*, Vol. 59, No. 1.

[31] Gottlieb, Scott (2014), "CBO: Obamacare is a tax on work, may cut full-time workforce by 2.5 million", *Forbes* (February 4). Retrieved from http://www.aei.org/article/health/cbo-obamacare-is-a-tax-on-work-may-cut-full-time-workforce/?utm_source=today&utm_medium=paramount&utm_campaign=020514#.UvJsWqhV5TM.email. In its new budget outlook, CBO very clearly states that Obamacare amounts to an implicit tax on work and workers that will reduce employment by as much as 2.5 million jobs over the next 10 years.

[32] Rosefielde, Steven and Mills, Quinn (2013). *Democracy and its Elected Enemies*, Cambridge: Cambridge University Press. Stewardship is generally recognized as the acceptance or assignment of responsibility to shepherd and safeguard the valuables of others, interpreted here as preserving national economic health and security.

Few, if any of the macro management policies advocated by contemporary government leaders are accidental. They all put insider interest first and the people's welfare last, despite misleading claims that representatives are the people's public servants useful for political coalition building.[33] Elsewhere, we have labeled the phenomenon "politocracy" in the American context, and defined it as a political economic system where leaders of big government, big business and big social advocacy jointly maximize their wealth and power by trafficking in public services while paying lip service to ideals and real public needs. The system's inner logic prioritizes expediency over efficiency and welfare, operating under the false banners of prosperity, full employment and social justice.[34]

Promises of prosperity, full employment and social justice are the facades; insider self-seeking is the reality.[35] The political posturing bamboozles many neoclassical economists who should know better, masking the need for radical economic reform. Witness the lost war on poverty where government miss incentives have perpetuated the problem despite the expenditures of trillions of dollars to eradicate it.[36]

---

[33] President Obama has issued more executive orders bypassing Congress and the Senate than all past presidents combined. Retrieved from http://www.whitehouse.gov/briefing-room/presidential-actions/executive-orders.

[34] The pre-Socratic philosopher Heraclitus used the term logos to describe an inner logic that can be perceived, but eludes ordinary comprehension.

[35] Lipton, Eric and Protess, Ben (2014), "Law Does not End Revolving Door on Capitol Hill", *New York Times* (February 2). Retrieved from http://dealbook.nytimes.com/2014/02/01/law-doesnt-end-revolving-door-on-capitol-hill/?_php=true&_type=blogs&hp&_r=0. Politicians and lobbyists collude in writing and interpreting legislation for mutual profit.

[36] Mathur, Aparna (2014), "In the War on Poverty, Cash Assistance will Fail", *AEI* (January 22). Retrieved from http://www.aei.org/article/economics/fiscal-policy/labor/in-the-war-on-poverty-cash-assistance-will-fail/?utm_source=today&utm_medium=paramount&utm_campaign=012214#.Ut_3i9YZzl0.email. Lyndon Johnson declared an unconditional war against poverty 50 years ago, but there are still 47 million Americans today classified as poor. Cf. CBO, *The Distribution of Household Income and Tax*, 2013. Retrieved from http://www.cbo.gov/sites/default/files/cbofiles/attachments/44604-AverageTaxRates.pdf. Saez, Emmanuel (2013), Striking it Richer: The Evolution of Top Incomes in the United States. Retrieved from http://elsa.berkeley.edu/~saez/saez-UStopincomes-2012.pdf.

Preventing another financial crisis, fending off decay and restoring robust global economic growth require the inclusive approach elaborated in subsequent chapters that identifies sources of secular stagnation,[37] and the causes of economic miss management including speculative excesses wrought by the willfulness and unscrupulousness of political insiders.

[37] Hoeller, Peter; Joumard, Isabelle and Koske, Isabell (2014), "Reducing Income Inequality While Boosting Economic Growth: Can it be Done? Evidence from OECD Countries", *The Singapore Economic Review*, Vol. 59, No. 1.

Chapter **3**

Insider Democracy

Most of us strive to maximize our productivity and efficiency because in doing so we earn the highest incomes, optimally accumulate wealth and consume over the course of our lives.[1] These good intentions may be thwarted by the market power of corporations or government dictate. Adam Smith showed more than two centuries ago that the losses caused by market power could be mitigated by free competition, and demonstrated that if government were kept in check, competitive markets would augment individual wealth and the wealth of nations.[2] Smith's formula for prosperity was rationality, business competition and responsible government.[3]

It worked admirably in the 18th century from some points of view, but the influence of Smith's doctrine waxed and waned thereafter.[4] Socialists

---

[1] Fisher, Irving (1930), *The Theory of Interest*, Clifton NJ: Augustus M. Kelley.

[2] Smith, Adam (1976), *Inquiry into the Nature and Causes of the Wealth of Nations*, London: W. Strahan and T. Cadell.

[3] Smith attacked all forms of government intervention in the private economy including protective tariffs and monopoly charters, but advocated state provision of other essential services including public education. *Wealth of Nations*, Book IV. Accordingly, he supported taxes to cover the cost of basic government services. Mark Blaug points out that Smith also saw good government as a device for realizing private sector potential. Blaug, Mark (1997), *Economic Theory in Retrospect*, Cambridge: Cambridge University Press, Chapter 2, Section 19, pp. 59–62.

[4] The world changed dramatically after 1776 when Adam Smith wrote the *Wealth of Nations*. It underwent an industrial revolution, a ceaseless technological revolution, a democratic

lauded the state, disparaged the market and insisted that individual preferences be restricted for the collective good. The Soviet Union, Mao's China,
Ho Chi Minh's Vietnam and Pol Pot's Cambodia carried this rejection of
Smith to extremes with well-known consequences. They criminalized
private ownership, business barter and entrepreneurship, replacing
markets with planning, directives, and state imposed incentives.[5] For a
time in the early postwar period, it seemed as if planning would supersede
markets everywhere,[6] but sentiment reversed in the late 1960s creating a
neoliberal illusion that unfettered competitive markets (*laissez faire*) were
the wave of the future.[7]

---

revolution, a secular cultural revolution, a communist revolution, a development revolu-
tion, an urbanization revolution, a social revolution, an occupational revolution, an educational revolution, a sexual revolution, a mass consumption revolution and a communications
revolution. The monarchical–aristocratic state Adam Smith perceived as a grave impedi-
ment to national prosperity vanished in the 20th century, together with innumerable educational, social and parochial barriers to labor mobility, democratic participation and
advancement. The devolution of authority initially empowered markets at the expense of
government and became synonymous with the concept of capitalist revolution. As the
market waxed, it seemed reasonable to suppose that state governance would wane. However,
the dark side of markets (monopoly power and crises) soon created new opponents who
looked to the state as a counterforce. The modern socialist movement began at the dawn of
the 19th century with a mixed agenda. Some like Robert Owen and Karl Marx sought to
criminalize markets, while others strove to capture the state from the old guard. Lenin and
his successors tried to do both, criminalizing private property, markets and entrepreneurship on one hand, and replacing it with state planning on the other.

 The twists and turns of this evolution including the rise of diverse non-socialist participatory elements do not concern us. The important point is it that the socialist movement set in motion a sequence of events that brought the state back from the brink of
irrelevance to position of dominance across the globe as the arbiter of entitlements.
National and transnational governmental reach are larger now than ever if one examines
their scope and detail. Governments dominate the media and the computer revolution has
enabled them to micro-regulate more aspects of ordinary life than the Soviets could with
their crude methods.

[5] Rosefielde, Steven (2007), *Russian Economy from Lenin to Putin*, New York, NY: Wiley.
[6] Feinstein, Charles (1975), *Socialism, Capitalism and Economic Growth: Essays Presented to
Maurice Dobb*, Cambridge: Cambridge University Press.
[7] Neoliberalism advocates economic liberalization, free trade, open markets, privatization
and deregulation. Williamson, John (2004), "A Short History of the Washington Consensus".
Retrieved from http://www.iie.com/publications/papers/williamson0904-2.pdf. Duménil,

This expectation however was disappointed. The abandonment of direct state control did not mean that government had ceded the field. The state merely decided to pursue its objective with indirect methods. There was no devolution of economic authority from the state to the private sector. Government did not restrict itself to being an efficient handmaiden to the market, or wither. It merely switched tactics in order to remain in command while simultaneously capturing some benefits of market place entrepreneurship and competition.

Sovereign Democracy

Government programs are bloated and continue to proliferate.[8] But instead of killing the goose that laid golden eggs as the Soviets did by replacing the private sector entirely with government run enterprises, today's politicians decided to gain advantage for political insiders (a caste, often referred to collectively as "the establishment")[9] in a different way. The new "enlightened conservative" system in Russia is called "sovereign democracy",[10] a term

---

Gerard and Lévy, Dominique (2013), *The Crisis of Neoliberalism*, Cambridge MA: Harvard University Press. Plant, Raymond (2009), *The Neo-Liberal State*, Oxford: Oxford University Press. Prasad, Monica (2006), *The Politics of Free Markets: The Rise of Neoliberal Economic Policies in Britain, France, Germany and the United States*, Chicago: University of Chicago Press. Jones, Daniel Stedman (2013), *Masters of the Universe: Hayek, Friedman and the Birth of Neoliberal Politics*, Princeton: Princeton University Press.

[8] Francis, David (2014), "DOD's $178 Billion Efficiency Plan a Total Failure", *The Fiscal Times* (January 23). Retrieved from http://www.thefiscaltimes.com/Articles/2014/01/23/DOD-s-178-Billion-Efficiency-Plan-Total-Failure. Three years ago, the Defense Department kicked off a program to improve efficiencies across the Pentagon. The plan was projected to save DOD some $178 billion over a five-year period. As of today, the program is a complete failure.

[9] This is an informal term seldom employed by academics. Norbert Elias and John Scotson (2009), *The Established and the Outsiders*, Dublin: University College.

[10] For a discussion of "enlightened conservatism" (prosveshchyonnyi conservatism) see Stanovaya, Tatiana (2014), "In Search of Lost Ideology", *Institute of Modern Russia* (April 25). Retrieved from http://www.imrussia.org/en/society/725-in-search-of-lost-ideology. "Alexander Shirinyants is known for writing extensively in his doctoral dissertation about the "possibility of forming a new ideology in Russia without adopting any Western models". He also emphasized the concept of "social conservatism, combining the patriotism and loyalty of cultural conservatism with the social idea of the right to a decent life, solidarity,

coined by Vladimir Putin and refined by Vladislav Surkov in 2006 to mislead naïve observers into believing that the Kremlin's authoritarian regime is governed by the people's will.[11]

The modern system in most parts of the globe like Putin's Russia leverages the benefits that big government programs offer political insiders by rent-granting (partnering) with the private sector, outsourcing, encouraging profit-seeking, and channeling private energies to suit the establishment's purposes, including obligations placed on people for political support and kickbacks.[12] The legions of "in-house" government bureaucrats changed little in the last few decades, but politicians' "outhouse" reach has vastly expanded, sounding the death knell for three crucial elements of a growing economy: Unfettered market competition, the Enlightenment concept of fostering rational self-interest,[13] and responsible government.[14]

---

and justice". The audience will be offered the doctrines of such ideologists of conservatism as Nikolai Berdyaev, Ivan Ilyin, Lev Tikhomirov, Nikolai Danilevski, Metropolitan Philaret (Drozdov), and Konstantin Pobedonostsev.

[11] Lipman, Masha (2006), "Putin's Sovereign Democracy", *Washington Post* (July 15). On "sovereign democracy" (suveryennaya demokratiya) see Vladislav Surkov, "Transcript of a speech by the Deputy Head of the Administration of the President of Russia, aide to the president of the Russian Federation, Vladislav Surkov for the center of partisan study and preparation of the staff of 'United Russian,'" February 7, 2006. According to Vladislav Surkov, sovereign democracy is: A society's political life where the political powers, their authorities and decisions are decided and controlled by a diverse Russian nation for the purpose of reaching material welfare, freedom and fairness by all citizens, social groups and nationalities, by the people that formed it. Surkov's "sovereign democracy" is not democratic at all because the leader governing society's political life decides what the people want, rather than the people doing it themselves through the ballot box.

[12] Rosefielde, Steven and Mills, Quinn (2013), *Democracy and its Elected Enemies: American Political Capture and Economic Decline*, Cambridge: Cambridge University Press. The problem is not confined to America. See Daley, Suzanne (2014), "So Many Bribes, a Greek Official Can't Recall Them All", *New York Times* (February 7). Retrieved from http://mobile.nytimes.com/2014/02/08/world/europe/so-many-bribes-a-greek-official-cant-recall-all.html?from=global.home.

[13] Rosefielde, Steven and Pfouts, Ralph W. (2014), *Inclusive Economic Theory*, Singapore: World Scientific Publishers.

[14] Lepore, Jill (2014), "The Warren Brief," *New Yorker* (April 21). Retrieved from http://www.newyorker.com/arts/critics/books/2014/04/21/140421crbo_books_lepore?currentPage=all. Congresswoman Elizabeth Warren contends in her new book "that the

Enterprises today cannot freely negotiate wages (because of minimum wages and diverse affirmative action mandates), terms and conditions of employment. They cannot avoid excessive government claims on their revenue (such as payroll taxes), profits and assets (inheritance and gift taxes). Corporate technologies, processes, products (types, assortments and characteristics) and investment options are all restricted by government prohibitions, mandates, executive orders, licensing and regulations, and are distorted too by subsidies, insurance guarantees and sundry enticements.[15] Marketing likewise is subject to pervasive regulations.

Income recipients and asset owners are not exempt from government interference. Few people receive what they earn or are able to shelter past accumulations from additional confiscation.[16] Anti-competitive government wage interventions (preferences and penalties), interest rate manipulations, unequal taxes, subsidies and transfers all contribute to warping consumer demand.

In a context of extensive and excessive government interference, the laws of competitive supply and demand cannot assure that autonomous individuals are rationally empowered to maximize their well-being because of the restrictions imposed by government on consumers' spending. The laws of competitive supply and demand do not protect people from — the market power of large firms when the government protects that power in a variety of ways. Nor can it be shown that

---

American political system places power in the hands of plutocrats and bankers at the expense of ordinary, middle-class Americans. "Big corporations hire armies of lobbyists to get billion-dollar loopholes into the tax system and persuade their friends in Congress to support laws that keep the playing field tilted in their favor", Warren writes. "Meanwhile, hardworking families are told that they will just have to live with smaller dreams for their children". This does not get said Larry Summers told her if she is going to be an insider "She could be an insider or an outsider, but if she was going to be an insider she needed to understand one unbreakable rule about insiders: 'They don't criticize other insiders.'"

[15] Christensen, Clayton M. and Bever, Derek van (2014), "The Capitalist's Dilemma", *Harvard Business Review* (June). Retrieved from http://hbr.org/2014/06/the-capitalists-dilemma/ar/1. The authors argue that pressure for quick returns is degrading long term investment. This is partly linked to financial liberalization.

[16] There are a variety of legitimate intergenerational transfer strategies that reduce the government's bite, but they are not panaceas, and for most people do not go much beyond tax free transfers to one's spouse.

government-rigged markets including the Organization of the Petroleum Exporting Countries (OPEC) are better than competitive market systems because the heart of the problem lies with government over-regulation,[17] not business's intrinsic under-competitiveness. The petroleum market underscores the claim. It is anti-competitively controlled by the insiders of 12 OPEC nations with the tacit collusion of non-OPEC oil producers, and private petroleum companies in league with their government officials. America until recently was awash with excess petroleum supplies that would lower prices domestically if the market were not anti-competitive, and would reduce prices abroad if the Obama administration vigorously pressed petroleum exports.[18] Instead, Washington withheld exportable petroleum surpluses as

---

[17]Government officials do not know what individuals want or need. They do not know how to efficiently satisfy individual demands, if somehow they miraculously knew them. Their values seldom are consonant with those of the people who elected them, and more often than not, they do not care. Governments now operate behind a façade of infallibility and compassion, but they are generally inept. The practical consequences of government ineptitude is that publically provided goods and services have the wrong characteristics, are over and under produced, and are maldistributed. That is, there is too much of some stuff; too little of other stuff; and whatever is produced does not end up where it does the most good. Moreover, public goods and services sheltered from competitive discipline are too costly because they are often produced with the wrong technologies, and overemploy and misemploy factors of production. Public goods and services are wasteful or "bads" when no one wants them. Their costs including "red tape" are invariably exorbitant. Worse still anti-competitive executive orders, Congressional mandates, set asides, pork barreling, logrolling and miss regulation warp private markets and distort work incentives. Scientific research and technological progress are retarded, entrepreneurship is chilled, market competition is impaired, corporate management is misdirected, effort is misguided and withheld, corruption is rife, and large segments of society are alienated. For a formal proof of these claims see Rosefielde, Steven and Pfouts, Ralph W. (2014), *Inclusive Economic Theory*, Singapore: World Scientific Publishers.

[18]James Woolsey former director of the CIA has argued for years that the OPEC juggernaut would be broken when new energy supplies of various sorts came online. Now that they have come online, the Obama administration has shown its true hand by failing to drive petroleum prices down. Woolsey, James (2012), "Destroying Oil's Monopoly and OPEC's Cartel". Retrieved from http://www.usesc.org/JRWGeopoliticsofEnergy0312.pdf.

national security reserves, a rationale that was no longer credible. The persistence of high petroleum prices at home and abroad until the Saudi's decided to drive shale oil producers out of business, therefore demonstrates that anti-competitiveness often is the hidden agenda of America's government officials.

The ubiquitous interference of government in the marketplace obscures objective assessments of government and business performance judged from the standpoint of competitive individual well-being, and allows officials to claim that they know what is best, have the power to accomplish it, and take all the right actions. The only exception that they admit is unforeseeable shocks like the dot.com collapse or the financial crises, even though they were predicted.

Most people understand that politicians' claims are twaddle, but suspend their disbelief because they hope that governments will mend their ways.[19] People are willing to subordinate reason to political authority heedless of the cost, just as their 18th century counterparts did. The result is that there are no well-defined limits placed on insider self-serving, including the president.[20] Thanks to the computer revolution, politicians today are able to compel businesses and citizens to supply more and more information to the government. This enables government to remotely manage and coerce many people to behave as they are instructed or incentivized. People are monitored, micro-mandated and induced to

---

[19] Economists steeped in the tradition of Adam Smith know that the wealth of nations depends more on markets than governments. Yet, when it comes to public policy, many double think. Even though economists teach their students that suppliers (including the state) should efficiently satisfy individual demand, they routinely endorse wasteful government programs, approve executive decrees that flout the rule of law, and support anti-competitive regulations that diminish the wealth of nations. All politicians have to do is declare a burning "need" and rational economy flies out the window. George Orwell coined the word in his dystopian novel "1984". Double think is a variant of newspeak that makes it blasphemous to oppose party dogma.

[20] Kuhnhenn, Jim (2014), "Obama orders to test workplace ideas", *Associated Press* (April 6). Retrieved from http://finance.yahoo.com/news/apnewsbreak-obama-orders-test-work-place-ideas-100157513--finance.html.

self-comply often under the threat of Draconian penalties.[21] George Orwell's tyrannical Big Brother would have approved.[22]

Politicians are supposed to serve the people (*public servants*), but due to their will to power, privilege and wealth have succeeded in turning the relationship between citizens and themselves topsy-turvy.[23] They have transformed most people into pawns in a governance game that allows insiders to flourish by pretending to advance social welfare.[24] The government then uses propaganda to assure enough people see matters its way to permit the process to continue. A façade of dissent, opposition and controversy about most issues is permitted, even welcomed. But there is a code of silence about politicians' usurpation of popular sovereignty via market capture and vacuous promises.[25]

The insider state has developed over recent decades with little or no potent opposition. Therefore, it is now running amok.[25] It is propagating

---

[21] For example, if you have an IRA, SEP, Simple IRA, 403(b) plan, 401(k) or other qualified retirement plan, you must begin taking distributions when you reach age 70-and-half. Missing a distribution carries a big penalty; 50% of the amount that was supposed to have been withdrawn is levied as an excise tax. Karlamangla, Soumya (2014), "Fear of penalty a reason for Obamacare's late surge in California", *Los Angeles Times* (April 4). Retrieved from http://www.latimes.com/business/healthcare/la-fi-mo-obamacare-penalty-20140401,0, 1930540.story#axzz2y7AKMO5r.

[22] George, Orwell (1949), *1984*, London: Secker and Warburg.

[23] "Ask not what your country can do for you, ask what you can do for your country". President John F. Kennedy, "Inaugural Address", January 20, 1961. It is the world of Gilbert and Sullivan's Mikado.

[24] Kupiec, Paul (2014), "Guess Who Makes More than Bankers: Their Regulators", *Wall Street Journal* (April 22). Retrieved from wsj.com/news/articles/SB10001424052702304311 204579507512375765276. "In 2012 at the Federal Deposit Insurance Corporation, the average pay was $190,000. At the Federal Reserve? It will not say".

[25] Some personal examples may be edifying. The government awarded a grant to the UNC Center for Slavic, Eurasian and East European Studies, but the travel part could not be used because a federal administrator had to approve flights to Europe. It took 30 day to obtain approval, and of course the flights were no long available when approved, and the fruitless process had to be repeated to no avail. Likewise, applying for a National Science Foundation (NSF) grant requires immense effort and resources to comply with trivial rules, but if there is any slip up, the grant is rejected without review. April 16, 2014, "Dear Campus Colleagues: We have experienced the 'rejection without review' of several NSF proposals due to non-compliance issues. These issues have all been in formatting — things that we

failed government programs and treating them as value added which is misleadingly included in calculations of economic growth. It is intensifying inefficiency and spawning financial crises.[26]

This is the reality of the new global political economy. It is not free enterprise, socialism, or communism; it is not conservative or liberal even though it is often defended on various idealistic grounds. Instead it is more like the 18th century aristocracy's revenge on Adam Smith. The new global political economy embraces the theory of Adam Smith and rejects its substance. Recognizing the substance of the new global political economy illuminates the challenges of preventing another financial crisis, restoring beneficial growth, fending off decay and dampening social discord.[27]

---

would have considered minor offenses in the past. Specific examples of how we have been cited for non-compliance include (by proposal section):

- Project Description: Not noting the terms "broader impacts" and "intellectual merit" in the section on previous NSF support;
- References Cited: Using the term "*et al*" instead of spelling out each author's name;
- Biosketches: That do not follow the NSF format to the letter;
- Supplemental Docs: Documentation not asked for in the NSF program solicitation included here has been seen as trying to circumvent the page limits. We conferred with NSF as to why we were no longer given the opportunity to make these minor corrections and heard about the high volume of proposals received by these NSF programs. We have also heard this week that Duke is having similar experiences with NSF. They were told outright by one NSF Program Officer that the PO was "being pressured to 'reduce the review burden' due to a high volume of submissions, and non-compliant proposals were a good place to start".

Lipton, Eric (2014), "Lobbyists, Bearing Gifts, Pursue Attorneys General", *New York Times*, October 28. Retrieved from http://www.nytimes.com/2014/10/29/us/lobbyists-bearing-gifts-pursue-attorneys-general.html.

[26] McFadden, Robert (2014), "Charles Keating, 90, Key Figure in '80s Savings and Loan Crisis, Dies", *New York Times* (April 2). Retrieved from http://mobile.nytimes.com/2014/04/02/business/charles-keating-key-figure-in-the-1980s-savings-and-loan-crisis-dies-at-90.html?referrer=.

[27] Historians call the 18th century west the age of absolutism to convey the notion that everyone was subordinated to the throne. Absolute monarchs however did not treat subjects equally. The nobility was a privileged co-governing estate that managed state affairs often for its own profit. Insiders for example had the throne grant them charters, that is, business monopolies both at home and in the colonies. Commoners were taxed to support both the nobility and the monarch. Adam Smith advocated the market as a device for circumscribing the scope of aristocratic privilege, aided by democratization. The strategy worked for a

Globalization today is not creating beneficial free markets for all, but instead is recreating the government-dominated and directed economic system of the Ancien Régime. The Ancien Régime benefited monarchs and the aristocracy. Its new incarnation benefits the establishment in each nation,[28] as well as their counterparts in transnational and international organizations.[29]

The new ruling caste claims to govern in everyone's interest, but does not do so. It governs in its own self-interest, and is inclined to over-reach with adverse consequences.[30] In the 18th century absolutism provided

---

while, but he failed to foresee that democratic representatives would soon covet the privileges of the discarded nobility.

[28] Those wishing to bribe public officials can easily find the right party with Horáková, Martina and Jordan, Amy (2014), *Directory of Financial Regulators 2014*, London: Central Banking Books.

[29] "China leaders' kin 'stash riches in offshore tax havens: Relatives of top Chinese leaders including President Xi Jinping and former premier Wen Jiabao have used offshore tax havens to hide their wealth, according to a mammoth investigation released on Wednesday". Retrieved from http://news.yahoo.com/chinese-leaders-39-kin-stash-riches-offshore-holdings-030944117.html.

[30] Carney, Timothy (2014), "K Street loses a loyal ally in Kathleen Sebelius", *Washington Examiner* (April 12). Retrieved from http://www.aei.org/article/politics-and-public-opinion/executive/k-street-loses-a-loyal-ally-in-kathleen-sebelius/?utm_source=today&utm_medium=paramount&utm_campaign=041414. By turning up at a party for a drug lobbyist during the Obamacare debate, Sebelius undermined President Obama's anti-lobbyist talk. Then again, Sebelius had done that already: Before entering politics, she ran a lobbying organization, the Kansas Trial Lawyers' Association. The revolving door always spun freely at Sebelius's Health and Human Service (HHS), in almost comically perfect ways.

HHS's top food cop is Michael Taylor, the former chief lobbyist for Monsanto. After Obamacare passed, Sebelius hired Liz Fowler to help put it into effect. Fowler was a revolving-door veteran who had alternated between the K Street-friendly office of Sen. Max Baucus and running the lobbying shop at insurance giant Wellpoint. Today, Fowler runs the lobby shop for pharmaceutical giant Johnson & Johnson. William Schultz, a top HHS lawyer hired by Sebelius, also came from K Street. Steering clear of Obama's "lobbyist bans", Schultz deregistered as a lobbyist in September 2008, and days later donated to Obama's campaign — while keeping at least some of his corporate clients until he joined HHS as deputy general counsel. Schultz's biggest client in his lobbying days was Barr Laboratories, maker of Plan B, the "morning-after pill". After Obamacare passed, Sebelius and Schultz's HHS construed the Obamacare provision on "women's preventive health"

snail-paced growth,[31] extreme inequity and violent revolution. The results today — despite greater possibilities — are apt to follow a similar script.

Most contemporary establishment-oriented economic and political analysts obfuscate the situation by addressing economic stagnation, inequality, and persistent unemployment without taking politicians' hidden agendas into account.[32] Summer's and Krugman's anti-austerity demand-side advocacy provides a case in point, but there are many rivals. Fingers are pointed at all the usual suspects: capitalists, entitlement advocates and bad policy. Everything is open to criticism except the new insider

---

as a requirement that employers cover 100% of the cost of all birth control, including Plan B. Sebelius promoted Schultz to general counsel in 2012 as that office took up cases defending the contraception mandate from religious-liberty lawsuits. To recap: A Monsanto lobbyist to regulate food, an insurance and drug lobbyist to implement Obamacare and a Plan B lobbyist to help mandate coverage of Plan B. Sebelius was a model of Obamanomics: Carrying plenty of sticks to drive industry where she wanted it to go and bushels of carrots to reward the compliant businesses. Drug companies benefitted from Sebelius's crafting of Obama's "Essential Health Benefits" rules, which were a prime culprit in outlawing many people's health plans. Late in the regulatory process, HHS responded to the drug lobby's requests and tweaked these rules, expanding the required drug coverage. Last week, Obama's HHS delayed the law's cuts to Medicare Advantage — cuts that were supposed to help fund the bill's subsidies for private insurance. Back in 2012, HHS also delayed these cuts — in a typically twisted fashion. Obamacare had (1) prescribed cuts in Medicare Advantage, and (2) set aside billions for HHS to conduct "demonstration projects" in how to expand health coverage. Sebelius's first "demonstration project" was undoing the Medicare Advantage cuts! Secretary Sebelius made sure to keep the insurers in line politically. After Obamacare passed, she warned insurers not to blame their premium increases on the law's slew of mandates. "There will be zero tolerance for this type of misinformation and unjustified rate increases", she wrote in late 2010. "Simply stated, we will not stand idly by as insurers blame their premium hikes and increased profits on the requirement that they provide consumers with basic protections. The revolving door. Abortion extremism. Disregard for the rule of law. Incompetent management. That's Sebelius's legacy. The secretary shall not be missed".

[31] Smith attributed British growth retardation to royalist political economy (sometimes obliquely described as mercantilism). Cf. Maddison, Angus (2003), *The World Economy: Historical Statistics*, Paris: OECD.

[32] Piketty, Thomas (2014), *Capital in the Twenty-First Century*, Cambridge MA: Harvard University Press. Piketty stresses the importance of politics in determining income inequality, but shuns any assessment of politicians complex motivations.

nobility.[33] Partisan wrangling aside, the establishment is treated as if it is beyond reproach and is a guarantor of brighter days.

Doctored Evidence

Today's aspiring aristocrats strive to preserve and expand their authority by controlling evidence of failure and by creating legitimizing myths or what Martin Malia calls ideocracy (soft ideology).[34] Statistics are massaged to support authorities' agendas.[35] This makes it difficult to assess economic

---

[33] Pfeiffer, Eric (2014), "Hard choices: Clintons rent 'modest' $18M Hamptons home for vacation", *Yahoo News* (August 8). Retrieved from http://news.yahoo.com/hard-choices--clintons-moving-to--modest---18m-hamptons-home-for-the-summer-154337464.html. "Still rebounding from criticism for insisting that she and Bill Clinton were 'dead broke' after leaving the White House, Hillary and Bill have decided to settle into 'modest' accommodations for the summer". "The couple has reportedly earned more than $100 million together since leaving the White House, with Hillary herself taking in millions in both speaking fees and contracts for her two best-selling books". "And after their summer vacation, if the Clintons are not trekking around the world on their various projects, they can always make a stop at one of the homes they do own, with residences in both New York and Washington DC. Their daughter Chelsea also resides in a Manhattan home reportedly worth $10.5 million".

[34] Malia, Martin (1994), *The Soviet Tragedy: A History of Socialism in Russia*, 1917–1991, New York NY: Free Press. Weber, Max (1978), *Economy and Society*, Berkeley CA: University of California Press. Rosefielde, Steven (1982), *False Science: Underestimating the Soviet Arms Buildup*, New Brunswick NJ: Transaction.

[35] Eberstadt, Nicholas (2014), "How the feds blind us to our malaise", *AEI* (April 10). Retrieved from http://www.aei.org/article/economics/fiscal-policy/how-the-feds-blind-us-to-our-malaise/?utm_source=today&utm_medium=paramount&utm_campaign=041014#.U0bT3rsRpL0.email. "Poverty and Social Mobility: 50 years into Washington's 'War On Poverty'", our government remains stunningly ill-equipped to offer hard information about either the prevalence of poverty and material deprivation or the chances of escaping from it. For nearly half a century, our main tool for tracking poverty in America has been a hastily-devised "federal poverty measure" unveiled in 1965 for calculating the nation's "poverty rate". This is not merely a bad yardstick — it is an awful one. It was designed in such a way that it cannot actually measure the living standards or spending power of the poor, focusing as it does on annual reported income rather than consumption. Suffice it to say that just about no one who follows the US poverty problem closely takes the "poverty rate" itself terribly seriously, for you cannot really tell if the true poverty situation is getting better or worse on the basis of these official annual soundings. "Welfare

performance and the risk of future crises.[36] Developing nations like China exaggerate gross domestic product (GDP) growth for a multiplicity of reasons and international statistical agencies dutifully incorporate corrupt official statistics into global economic data series.[37] Banks disguise bad debts

---

Dependency: Long-term entitlement dependency in America is a worry to policy-makers on both sides of the aisle. The US government currently spends about $1 trillion a year on 'means-tested' anti-poverty programs. How many people avail themselves of those benefits today-and how many are year-in, year-out dependents on them? For answers, we have to consult the data from SIPP, the aforementioned statistical waif within the Census Bureau family. SIPP was specifically devised to provide this sort of information-that is the 'Program Participation' referred to in its acronym. Go to its website, you can get that information right up to the year 2011. No, that is not a typo. Take a look at the website: Right now you cannot find anything beyond the Fourth Quarter of 2011. That's what: Ten quarters out of date? Call it two and a half years. At that pace, we would not be learning about our present entitlement situation until almost 2017". "Family Breakdown: As everybody knows, modern America is suffering a crisis of the family. The increasing fragility of the family structure in the US has direct ramifications not only for the children and parents in question, but for society as a whole. Consequently, for going on two decades, the detailed information necessary for reckoning our national marriage rate and divorce rate are simply no longer on the grid. That is right: Our 'deciders' decided to jettison such information as extraneous at precisely the point when it may matter most to our nation, and to our future".

[36] Rosefielde, Steven and Mills, Quinn (2012), "Global Default", in Steven Rosefielde, Masaaki Kuboniwa and Satoshi Mizobata, eds., *Prevention and Crisis Management: Lessons for Asia from the 2008 Crisis*, Singapore: World Scientific.

[37] Maddison's OECD statistics still report that Cambodian GDP grew at 6.7% per annum 1975–1979, at a time when more than 20% of the population and a larger share of the able bodied labor forces was decimated in Pol Pot's killing fields! Cf. Scissors, Derek (2014), China's GDP Growth Says Little", *AEI* (January 21). Retrieved from http://www.aei.org/article/economics/international-economy/chinas-gdp-growth-says-little/?utm_source=today&utm_medium=paramount&utm_campaign=012214#.UuAAe6cQft8.email. "James Rickards, in his new book "The Death of Money", offers an explanation for the country's surfeit of non-productive investment and a further warning for investors in China, estimating that actual Chinese GDP growth adjusted for the cost of mal-investment and corruption may be half the official rate. Visitors to China are often struck by the sight of huge real estate developments sitting unoccupied, roads and bridges going unused, and other examples of state-sponsored overcapacity". John Kahn (2014), "China's Turn For A Debt Crisis: Keep Your Eyes Open For The Unexpected", *Forbes* (June 12). Retrieved from http://www.forbes.com/sites/jamescahn/2014/06/12/chinas-turn-for-a-debt-crisis-keep-your-eyes-open-for-the-unexpected/?partner=yahootix._Rickards, James (2014), *The Death of Money: The Coming Collapse of the International Monetary System*, New York NY: Portfolio Hardcover.

and credit rating agencies play along. Much of this doctoring is intentional or acquiescent. However, the distortion is compounded by the serendipity of "hidden inflation".[38]

Hidden inflation was familiar to citizens of the Soviet Union. It is now, unfortunately, infecting western democracies. It is the over-reporting of economic growth by incorrectly treating government misspending, abusive mandates (which are a form of forced substitution for consumers and businesses), executive orders and rigged market transactions as real value added in official national income accounts.[39]

The process of hidden inflation works this way: Governments directly or indirectly fix prices like postal, health, educational and environmental

---

[38] Hidden inflation is a term used to describe inflation concealed by statistical trickery that falsely reports price changes as output growth. This occurs whenever price authorities for a multitude of reasons wrongly judge that increases in sale prices are justified by commensurate improvements in product quality, prompting statistical authorities to enter the change in national income accounts as output gains (better quality) instead of inflation. Inflation is inflation, but not only can it be partially concealed, it can be statistically miss portrayed as economic growth. Soviet managers were masters of this dark art. They used to introduce "new" products at higher prices, claiming that mark ups were justified by enhanced value added, when they merely poured old wine into new bottles. "Red directors" as they were called would add a star to the cognac label and double the price without altering the product. They did this because bonuses were tied to profits, and "hidden inflation" provided them with easy rewards. Their behavior was criminal, but authorities treated it as a victimless crime because "hidden inflation" increased the Soviet Union's GDP growth rate. If the state cracked down on wayward managers Soviet leaders would have been compelled to report that the economy had been stagnant during the entire decade before it collapsed. Rosefielde, Steven (2007), *Russian Economy from Lenin to Putin*, New York NY: Wiley.

[39] Hidden inflation is any price increase that is disguised by mischaracterizing it as valued added (quantity/or quality) in national income accounting. When the government compels people to buy services that are not needed, or increases the prices of these unnecessary services, the cost is treated as value added in national income accounting. But these costs should not be treated this way because in fact the extra expenditure is a pure price increase. The same principle applies to taxation. Supposedly the taxes people pay provide them with value added (public services). If taxes are increased, but no additional services are provided, this again is hidden inflation. Increases in rents are equivalent to hidden inflation when they are not demand justified. The public does not think through the word tax carefully enough. Tax increases can be justified if they provide real value added, but otherwise they are unjustified. Justified tax increases augment value added. Unjustified tax increases are pure inflation. The point is important for understanding how misleading nature of the government component of GDP.

services and continuously increase them pretending that the increases are justified by rising competitive costs or quality improvements.[40] Increases in government waste, fraud and abuse, including ObamaCare and "clean energy",[41] as well as the diversion of resources from the private to the public sector then appear in national income accounts as economic growth,[42] instead of being properly deducted as diminished economic welfare. Government misconduct in this way becomes win–win for insiders. Politicians have their way, and transmute failures like those now apparent in higher education into statistical successes.[43]

---

[40] The state sets reimbursement rates for Medicare and Medicaid that serve as insurance benchmarks. Service providers then pad their bills to justify rate increases, with government review boards determining the "permissible" rates Soviet style of hidden inflation.

[41] Zycher, Benjamin (2014), "'Cleantech' Gets Clocked By 60 Minutes, and the Usual Suspects Try to Make Lemonade", *AEI* (January 23). Retrieved from http://american.com/archive/2014/january/cleantech-gets-clocked-by-60-minutes-and-the-usual-suspects-try-to-make-lemonade?utm_source=today&utm_medium=paramount&utm_campaign=012314. "Despite massive taxpayer-funded subsidies, 'clean energy' is a failure because it remains far too expensive to compete in the marketplace. "Cleantech" is the sanitized term for this broad array of subsidized energy technology beneficiaries: Firms producing batteries, solar devices, wind power components, "efficient" autos, "alternative" electricity, "renewable" electric generating facilities, ad infinitum. Together with "clean" and "renewable". Cleantech is a word that obscures the less-than-clean, life-or-death tug of war among interest groups competing for snout privileges at the federal "clean energy" trough. The term hides the unreported reality that there is little "clean" about "clean energy": It has environmental advantages over conventional energy only if we ignore the adverse environmental effects of "clean energy". The reality is that "clean energy" simply is very costly and uneconomic — in a word, uncompetitive — due to the inherently unconcentrated energy content of sunlight and wind flows, due to their intermittent availability and thus their unreliability, and due to the difficulty of sharp improvements in battery technology. And due to the vast increase in natural gas supplies and the resulting decline in prices brought by advances in horizontal drilling and hydraulic fracturing. After "$100 billion in loans, grants, and tax breaks ... [Cleantech] suffered a string of expensive tax-funded flops". "Clean and renewable" energy has proven so costly and so uncompetitive that even the Europeans are backing away from their own mandates rapidly".

[42] Adam Smith called this a diversion of resources from productive to unproductive use. Campbell, R.H. and Skinners, S.S. (1981), *The Glasgow Edition of the Works and Correspondence of Adam Smith*, Indianapolis: Liberty Fund, Vol. 2(A), p. 10.

[43] Official Soviet statistics reported rapid GDP growth virtually up to end when secular stagnation brought the system to its knees. These statistics lent credibility to the claim that

Straitjacket Government

Smith's grievance against the British economic governance system was that it coddled privilege and was intrinsically inefficient.[44] This is exactly what today's global economic system is doing. Over the centuries claims to entitlement have diversified, and insider access has been partly democratized, but this has not stopped privilege from becoming increasingly stultifying when evaluated from the perspective of competitive economic potential. An immense portion of the world's labor force is directly and

---

the Communist Party of the Soviet Union (CPSU) faithfully and successfully advanced the people's welfare, when insiders actually did what they pleased, plausibly imagining like North Korea's Kim Jong-un today that they could get away without it forever. See Rosefielde, Steven (2007), *Russian Economy from Lenin to Putin*, New York NY: Wiley. Keierleber, Mark (2014), "Business and Academic Leaders Disagree on Quality of College Graduates, Surveys Find", *Chronicle of Higher Education* (February 25). Retrieved from http://chronicle.com/article/BusinessAcademicLeaders/144977/?cid=pm&utm_source=pm&utm_medium=en. Do graduates have the skills they need to succeed on the job? Just 11% of business leaders, but 96% of academic leaders, strongly agree.

[44] *Wealth of Nations*, Book I, Chapter 7, Paragraph 26. "A monopoly granted either to an individual or to a trading company has the same effect as a secret in trade or manufactures. The monopolists, by keeping the market constantly understocked, by never fully supplying the effectual demand, sell their commodities much above the natural price, and raise their emoluments, whether they consist in wages or profit, greatly above their natural rate. The price of monopoly is upon every occasion the highest which can be got. The natural price, or the price of free competition, on the contrary, is the lowest which can be taken, not upon every occasion, indeed, but for any considerable time together. The one is upon every occasion the highest which can be squeezed out of the buyers, or which, it is supposed, they will consent to give: The other is the lowest which the sellers can commonly afford to take, and at the same time continue their business". *Wealth of Nations*, Book I, VIII. "We rarely hear, it has been said, of the combinations of masters, though frequently of those of workmen. But whoever imagines, upon this account that masters rarely combine, is as ignorant of the world as of the subject. Masters are always and everywhere in a sort of tacit, but constant and uniform, combination, not to raise the wages of labor above their actual rate [...] Masters, too, sometimes enter into particular combinations to sink the wages of labor even below this rate. These are always conducted with the utmost silence and secrecy till the moment of execution; and when the workmen yield, as they sometimes do without resistance, though severely felt by them, they are never heard of by other people". In contrast, when workers combine, "the masters [...] never cease to call aloud for the assistance of the civil magistrate, and the rigorous execution of those laws which have been enacted with so much severity against the combination of servants, laborers, and journeymen".

indirectly employed in what Smith considered unproductive and counter-productive labor. Straitjacket government prohibits some productive activities, hogties others, suffocates competitive scientific research, impedes entrepreneurship, embeds inequality, and shrivels productive investment.[45] Official hidden inflation-ridden statistics blur the picture by exaggerating economic growth, but in the absence of optimal regulation, miss-regulated outcomes must always be inferior.[46]

Secular stagnation does not just happen. It is brought about by insiders strangling internal and external competitive processes. Figure 3.1 provides an overview of the problem. It illustrates the Soviet administrative command planning system, but can easily be reinterpreted to describe any multi-industrial conglomerate, or a western mixed economy. The organization chart is divided into three columns, all subsumed under a central authority: The Soviet state economic directorate, conglomerate CEO or President Obama. The basic information essential for planning production and investment is gathered and processed by a central planning agency (Office of Management and Budget, which is part of the White House) and sent to the central authority. These suggested plan objectives are advisory and can be altered by the supreme authority to suit his/her taste. The middle column outlines the executive apparatus starting with the Council of Economic Ministers (divisional heads or cabinet) immediately beneath the leader, and then proceeding down the chain of command to supervisory departments overseeing production, factor acquisition and output distribution. Authority over statistics, planning and production is internal. Both the Soviet system and contemporary conglomerates were/are self-sufficient and did not/do not need markets to operate. They were/are able to coordinate production internally through plans, directives, contracts and bank oversight of monetary payments for wages and sales. The same principle

---

[45] Roubini, Nouriel (2014), "Slow Growth and Short Tails", *Project Syndicate* (January 22). Retrieved from http://digital@project-syndicate.org. "There is a looming risk of secular stagnation in many advanced economies, owing to the adverse effect on productivity growth of years of underinvestment in human and physical capital".

[46] Fitzgerald, Sandy (2014), "Taxpayer Tab for 4 State Obamacare Exchanges: $474 Million and Counting", *NewsMax* (May 11). Retrieved from ront/obamacare-state-exchangesfailures/2014/05/11/id/570677/?ns_mail_uid=68131196&ns_mail_job=1568704_05112014&promo_code=kvcnbjfq.

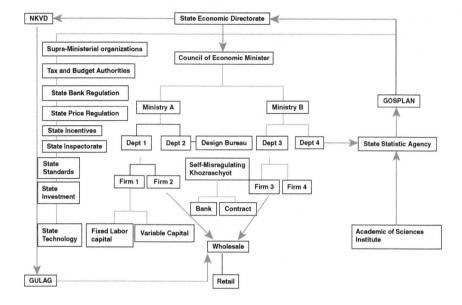

Figure 3.1.   Soviet planning and supply administration mechanism.

applies to the production of public services in America, whether or not markets are employed on an ancillary basis.[47]

The third column in Figure 3.1 illustrates the Soviet regulatory mechanism. The Soviet Union controlled product standards, occupational safety and health, prices, wages, bank and financial regulation, incentives, taxes, subsidies, and monetary policy. It financed new technologies and investment. This regulatory apparatus also applies in the west guiding, ordering, mandating and otherwise compelling conglomerates and all other market participants to modify their internal and market behavior in compliance with government desires.

---

[47] The Soviet Union did this 1921–1929 and 1987–1991; conglomerates routinely compete with other corporations in the market place, and contemporary governments outsource. Freeman, Jody and Minow, Martha (eds.) (2009), *Government by Contracting: Outsourcing and Democracy*, Cambridge MA: Harvard University Press. In 2008 more than 5 million private sector workers were employed as US government outsources, at a cost of $500 billion. Kenny, Charles (2013), "Why Private Contractors Are Lousy at Public Services", *Bloomberg Businessweek* (October 28). Retrieved from http://www.businessweek.com/articles/2013-10-28/outsourcing-can-be-a-lousy-alternative-to-government-run-services.

The history of command communism teaches that the tighter government control in the middle and far left columns (managerial strait-jacketing), the more poorly the supply system performs, even before taking account of the extent to which supplies satisfy consumer demands.[48] This lesson should apply as well to any overregulated system regardless of ownership and market opportunities.

Financial Crises

Many of us are willing to spend other people's money much more liberally than we are willing to spend our own. Politicians are no exception. Today's government insiders and their allies carry the attitude to extremes. They pile on debt and recklessly print money, while simultaneously thwarting growth essential for debt repayment.[49] This is the syndrome that drove the 2008 global financial crisis, inured inequality, and stands as the primary driver of mega-crises to come.

The perils of excessive government spending and credit creation are compounded by the demise of competitive markets at the hands of the usurping state, but crises, stagnation and decay are mostly misinterpreted by analysts as the triumph of private sector greed over efficient government. This topsy-turvy misdiagnosis increases the danger. While Summers and Krugman attempt to blame the risks of economic turmoil on short-sighted government retrenchment and austerity, they disregard the realities of contemporary state economic miss governance.[50] The most likely

---

[48] Rosefielde, Steven (2010), *Red Holocaust*, London: Routledge.

[49] The counterargument is that economic growth is endogenously determined by government support for science. Romer, David (2011), "Endogenous Growth", in *Advanced Macroeconomics* (4th edn.), New York NY: McGraw-Hill, pp. 101–149. Barro, Robert J. and Sala-i-Martin, Xavier (1995), *Economic Growth*, New York NY: McGraw-Hill. Cf. Krugman, Paul (2013), "The New Growth Fizzle", *New York Times* (August 18). Krugman, Paul (2013), "Bubbles, Regulation, and Secular Stagnation", *New York Times* (September 25). Retrieved from http://krugman.blogs.nytimes.com/2013/09/25/bubbles-regulation-and-secular-stagnation. Makin, John (2014), "Can policy boost growth?" *AEI* (January 7). Retrieved from http://www.aei.org/outlook/economics/can-policy-boost-growth/?utm_source=today&utm_medium=paramount&utm_campaign=010714.

[50] This dual solution does not dispose of the debt baby, but here too there is the promise of a free lunch, this time via government fostered productivity growth in accordance with endogenous economic growth theory.

outcome of expanding entitlements, encouraging under-saving and personal indebtedness, imposing more progressive taxes, doubling the minimum wage, squeezing the middle class, abusing affirmative action, prioritizing Black and Hispanic retirees, increasing government control over private education and fostering socially undesirable technological change,[51] is that their strategy will backfire for most citizens.

Summers and Krugman refuse to concede anything to Adam Smith, even though both claim to share "supply-side" concerns about stultifying anticompetitive aspects of government programs and management,[52] bemoan inequality,[53] and fret about the dangers of another financial crisis. Their anti-Smithian strategy dovetails perfectly with insiders' "bigger is always better" agenda,[54] creating a synergy that makes a mockery of their stated intent to combat inequality, crisis and decay.[55]

---

[51] See Chapter 1. Schwab, Klaus (2014), "The Global Economy in 2014", *Project Syndicate* (January 22). Retrieved from digital@project-syndicate.org. "Ultimately, however, the path to sustained growth requires not just new policies, but also a new mindset. Our societies must become more entrepreneurial, more focused on establishing gender parity, and more rooted in social inclusion. There simply is no other way to return the global economy to a path of strong and sustained growth".

[52] Summers, Lawrence (2013), "Washington Must Not Settle for Secular Stagnation", *Financial Times* (December 5). Retrieved from http://www.ft.com/cms/s/2/ba0f1386-7169-11e3-8f92-00144feabdc0.html#ixzz2pi6xfiEe.

[53] Carney, Timothy (2014), "Obama subsidizes private jets for high-flyers abroad", *AEI* (April 2). Retrieved from http://www.aei.org/article/politics-and-public-opinion/obama-subsidizes-private-jets-for-high-flyers-abroad/?utm_source=today&utm_medium=paramount&utm_campaign=040214#.Uzwy_0qmRsk.email. "The Export–Import Bank of the US recently announced a milestone: Under Obama, the agency has subsidized the sale of $1 billion in private jet sales to overseas customers".

[54] Rosencranz, Charles (2010), "Bigger is Better: The Case for a Transpacific Economic Union", *Foreign Affairs*, Vol. 89, No. 3, pp. 42–51.

[55] Malpass, David (2014), "How Big Government Drives Inequality: Stifling Economic Growth and Benefiting Insiders with Washington Access do not Help the Middle Class", *Wall Street Journal* (January 15). Retrieved from http://online.wsj.com/news/article_email/SB10001424052702303848104579312422581164580-lMyQjAxMTA0MDEwNjExNDYyWj. Rampton, Roberta (2014), "Obama targets poverty in San Antonio, Philadelphia and other U.S. 'zones'" (January 8). Retrieved from http://www.reuters.com/article/2014/01/08/us-usa-obama-jobs-idUSBREA070O820140108. Obama signaled last month that he plans a new focus this year on income inequality, which he called "the defining challenge of our time", pushing to raise the minimum wage and find new ways to help poor children break out of the cycle of poverty. As part of this effort, Obama will create "promise zones".

Chapter **4**

Squeezing the Middle Class

"All animals are equal, but some animals are more equal than others".

George Orwell
Animal Farm

Them Against Us

There is an important historical precedent for today's predicament. By see-ing what happened yesterday, we may glimpse tomorrow's possibilities. At the end of the Enlightenment, the French Revolution displaced the Ancien Régime's monarchy and privileged estates: the first estate of the clergy, and the second estate of the nobility.[1] The first estate represented the divine. The second estate composed of knights of the realm, was the nation's sword and shield. Historical precedent exempted both estates from paying taxes.[2] As popular upheavals approached and the ancient régime tottered, the third estate (commoner stakeholders) perceived itself as sheep being sheared for the benefit of the monarch, nobility and clergy — the establishment of their time. Many people, including finance minister Jacques Necker warned the crown of the danger of popular unrest and proposed reforms to preserve the

---

[1] On August 4, 1789 after a series of peasant revolts, the National Constituent Assembly abolished feudalism.

[2] Segments of the urban business community while formally obligated to pay taxes success-fully evaded them through various loopholes. Everyone else who could be squeezed paid.

feudal system.[3] The first and second estates however were unwilling to relinquish their privileges; they hung on until forcibly dispossessed.

Similarly today the dangers posed by financial crises are not being taken to heart, and warnings of popular unrest are falling on deaf ears.

Insiders nowadays are confident that the people can always be gulled into believing that the interests of the establishment and those of outsiders are the same. Insiders are complacent and cannot imagine being dethroned. They are wrong.[4] While it is true that the composition of today's estates has changed and that there is considerable inter-estate social mobility, this has not alleviated social restiveness. Victims are keenly aware that they are being coerced, that their living standards are declining and horizons darkening. They are gradually realizing that glib promises may not be enough to overcome secular stagnation; prevent another financial crisis and forestall decay. Some are beginning to recognize that the only solution may lie in completing the unfinished business of the French Revolution.

The Beleaguered Middle Class

The combustibility of the contemporary situation will depend on the rapaciousness of the establishment, the reaction of its victims, and external events just as it did during the Ancien Régime. There is little doubt on the

---

[3] Intellectuals like Voltaire fanned the flames of revolution by descrying religious and secular inequities. "He is remembered and honored in France as a courageous polemicist who indefatigably fought for civil rights (as the right to a fair trial and freedom of religion) and who denounced the hypocrisies and injustices of the Ancien Régime. The Ancien Régime — according to common opinion — involved an unfair balance of power and taxes between the three Estates: clergy and nobles on one side, the commoners and middle class, who were burdened with most of the taxes, on the other". *Wikipedia.*
[4] Pylas, Pan (2014), "Survey Finds Distrust in Government Growing", *USA Today* (January 20). Retrieved from http://www.usatoday.com/story/news/world/2014/01/20/distrust-in-government-growing/4655111/. "The 2014 Edelman Trust Barometer found the largest-ever gap in its 14-year history — 14 points — between trust in government and trust in business". "This is a profound evolution in the landscape of trust from 2009, where business had to partner with government to regain trust", agency CEO Richard Edelman said. He warned that sinking trust in government could stoke a rise in support for more extreme political parties, particularly in May's election for the European Parliament".

first score. Self-seeking political insiders and their associates in the private sector are prepared to press their personal interests against anyone who stands in their way. The risk of violent discord therefore hinges on whether today's beleaguered middle class (new working class) can be reasonably likened to the 18th century's third estate in a combustible environment.

The resemblance albeit imperfect is nonetheless close in its essentials. The third estate under the Ancien Régime included all citizens excluded from the first and second estate. Members were collectively viewed as commoners, and comprised 97% of the population. The category covered men with diverse livelihoods including peasants (serfs), independent land-owning farmers, guild masters, apprentices, journeymen, merchants, wage workers, financiers, professionals, public administrators and civil servants. Women were classified by their relationship to their "lords" (father or husband) rather than their economic role in the workplace. The status of fringe elements beyond the society's pale was inexplicit, perhaps because non-productive elements were not considered stakeholders.

The peasantry (serfs) constituted the vast majority of the third estate. They together with day laborers were mostly poor. Some independent farmers, and many guild masters, merchants, financiers, professionals, and civic administrators were affluent. During the middle ages the wealthy stratum of urban guild masters, merchants, financiers, professionals and civic administrators were described collectively as the bourgeoisie, and treated as a middle class on socio-economic grounds (as distinct from their estate status) occupying a space between the nobility and the poor. At the time of the French Revolution the concept of bourgeoisie was re-conceptualized to mean capitalist; that is, a wealthy business class whose fortune and interests were tied to commercial and financial assets rather than hereditary land ownership. They gradually became thought of not as part of the third estate, but as an affluent insurgent class and ultimately the successor to the privileged nobility.

The defining characteristics of the third estate circa 1789 taking these various nuances into account were productive labor and tax liability, not living standards or moderate wealth. The third estate was aggrieved at the feudal system because although the Ancien Régime provided a framework for stable productive activity, it overtaxed commoners to support the clergy and indulge the indolent nobility. The social order pitted the privileged against the productive third estate (mostly working poor). It degenerated into a confrontation between them and us, stoking the flames of revolutionary indignation.

Today's middle class as the term is now commonly understood has affinities with the Ancien Régime's third estate. Its members are socio-economically heterogeneous, and comprise the vast majority of the population, encompassing people from diverse walks of life: agricultural day workers, independent farmers, corporate farmers, craftsman, apprentices (interns), merchants, small businessmen, industrialists, blue and white collar wage workers, salaried personnel, financiers, professionals and civil servants. All members have formal legal rights, and corresponding tax obligations.

However, there are important differences between the third estate and the modern middle class. Contemporary women are classified primarily by their income and wealth, rather than their husband's rank; work status is subsidiary, and the middle excludes both the rich and the poor. It is defined primarily by income and wealth criteria; rather than the role or lack thereof that members play in the productive process.

The most important consequence of these evolutionary changes is that the tax burden has shifted jointly from productive commoners to the rich and productive middle class with the ability to pay out of their passive and earned incomes. Able bodied individuals not working for diverse reasons (including many feigning disabilities) and low wage earners including some clergy do not pay income taxes,[5] and are mostly subsidized. The productive taxpayers in the new working class (middle class) are blue and white collar wage earners; salaried personnel, and the self-employed defined here as most individual service providers, small and medium size proprietors, and middle income professionals.

In today's America nearly half of all households required to report wages, interest and capital gains to federal authorities pay no federal income tax. This is not misleading. It is a fact.[6] The burden of supporting

---

[5] In America workers including the self-employed pay Social Security taxes and Medicare taxes. Self-employed individuals pay twice as much as individual workers, plus unemployment taxes. Everyone pays sales tax.

[6] Sometimes the fact is obliquely disputed by noting that everyone pays sales tax. Sales tax is a separate matter. Nearly half of all income recipients in America do not pay

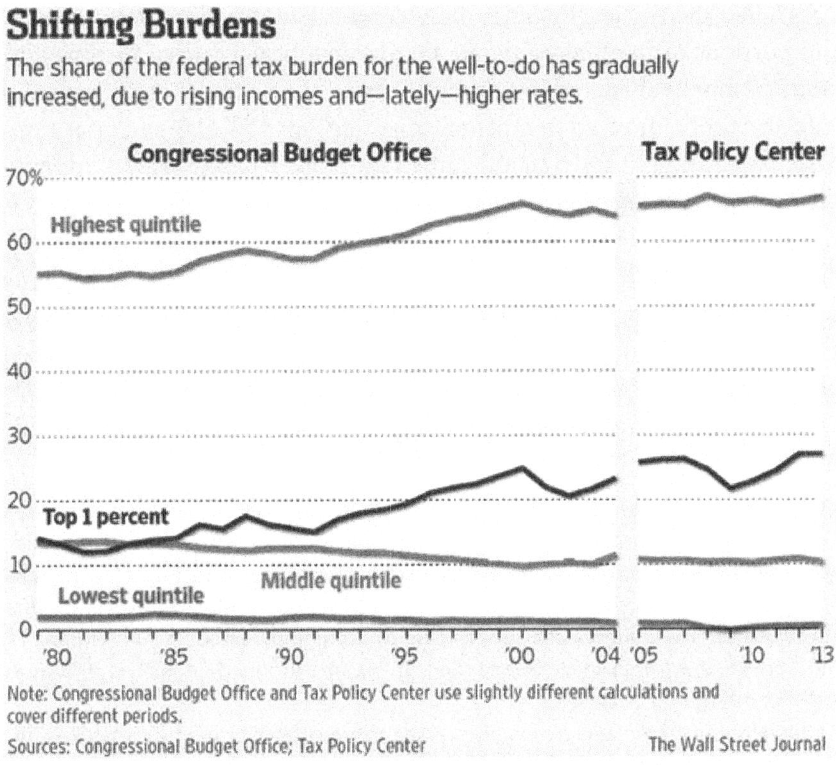
Shifting Burdens
The share of the federal tax burden for the well-to-do has gradually increased, due to rising incomes and—lately—higher rates.
Congressional Budget Office
Tax Policy Center
70%
60
50
40
30
20
10
0
Highest quintile
Top 1 percent
Middle quintile
Lowest quintile
'80
'85
'90
'95
'00
'04
'05
'10
'13
Note: Congressional Budget Office and Tax Policy Center use slightly different calculations and cover different periods.
Sources: Congressional Budget Office; Tax Policy Center
The Wall Street Journal

Figure 4.1. Tax burden on the productive middle class.

the poor and subsidizing big business consequently is loaded on the other half (Figure 4.1),[7] that is, the new working class and wealthy asset holders.[8]

---

federal income tax. See Thompson, Derek (2014), "How America Pays Taxes — in 10 Not-Entirely-Depressing Charts", *The Atlantic* (April 16). Retrieved from http://finance.yahoo.com/news/america-pays-taxes-10-not-130000290.html.

[7] Pethokoukis, James (2014), "Do liberals really think an 80% top tax rate wouldn't hurt the US economy?" *AEI* (April 14). Retrieved from http://www.aei-ideas.org/2014/04/do-liberals-really-think-80-tax-rate-would-be-ok/?utm_source=today&utm_medium=paramount&utm_campaign=041514.

[8] Rosefielde, Steven and Mills, Quinn (2013), *Democracy and its Elected Enemies*, Cambridge: Cambridge University Press.

Unlike the Ancien Régime, the second estate (wealthy asset holders) and portions of the first estate are taxed, often heavily when income and assets cannot be sheltered by corporate forms of ownership and nominally "not-for-profit" non-governmental organizations (NGOs) and charities.[9] Also, estate and gift taxes significantly reduce inheritable wealth,[10] despite the counter-influence of revocable and non-revocable living trusts.[11]

Accordingly, the core of the nation's productive workers, primarily those in the middle class with family incomes above $50,000 per year, is continuously being pressured to support the anti-productive governing establishment and swelling ranks of unproductive people (retirees, unemployed, and dependents, including those feigning disabilities),[12] across the income spectrum.[13] Funding is extracted from the productive

---

[9] Raymond, Nate (2014), "Texas' Wyly brothers committed fraud, U.S. jury finds", *Reuters* (May 12). "Texas businessman Samuel Wyly and the estate of his deceased brother, Charles, were liable for fraud for having engaged in a "scheme of secrecy" involving offshore trusts that netted them $550 million in trading profits, a jury decided on Monday". Retrieved from http://finance.yahoo.com/news/texas-wyly-brothers-committed-fraud-165329941.html.

[10] In America, the marginal federal estate and gift tax after the first $6 million is 40%. Most states levy additional estate taxes.

[11] http://www.americanbar.org/content/dam/aba/migrated/publiced/practical/books/wills/chapter_5.authcheckdam.pdf.

[12] Roy, Avik (2014), "White House: It's A Good Thing that Obamacare will Drive 2.5 Million Americans Out of the Workforce", *Forbes* (February 5), http://www.forbes.com/sites/theapothecary/2014/02/05/white-house-its-a-good-thing-that-obamacare-will-drive-2-5-million-americans-out-of-the-workforce/?partner=yahootix. "Press Secretary Jay Carney claimed that 2.5 million Americans leaving the workforce was a good thing, because they would no longer be 'trapped in a job'". The Democratic Party has historically championed subsidies like unemployment insurance that reduce the incentive to work. Carney's comment reflects the predisposition. It can be inferred that if the administration could, it would have the rich (household gross personal income above $200,000) provide the transfers required that would allow everyone else to work only as much as he or she desired. Once upon a time, savers were thought to be essential for vibrant economic growth, now the prudent middle class, retirees and passive rich are viewed as sitting ducks for forced low interest rates and inflation taxes.

[13] Pethokoukis, James (2014), "Do liberals really think an 80% top tax rate would not hurt the US economy?" *AEI* (April 14). Retrieved from http://www.aei-ideas.org/2014/04/do-liberals-really-think-80-tax-rate-would-be-ok/?utm_source=today&utm_medium=paramount&utm_campaign=041514. "Citing the CBO, the WSJ notes that "the increase in

class as illustrated in Figure 4.1 by excessive income taxation, but also by the skewed burden of payroll taxes (Federal Insurance Contributions Act (FICA) and Self Employed Contributions Act (SECA)), open inflation,[14] hidden inflation, mandates, executive orders and deferred debt obligation that the new working class ultimately will be forced to pay.[15]

This system is less blatantly exploitive than the Ancien Régime because rich successors to the second estate pay a significant portion of the tax bill, some of which goes Robin Hood style to the poor (and untouchables),[16] but appearances are deceptive. The burden on today's core taxable productive middle class is far greater and unjust than under the Ancien Régime because fewer and fewer have to support a larger group of privileged claimants,[17] and the American government revenue collection practices are increasing flouting due process.[18] All animals rich, poor and middle are

---

the individual income tax burden borne by the top 20% — such as couples with two children making more than $150,000 — has gone from 65% in 1980 to more than 90% as of 2010". This shows that the upper middle class is being hit. "I suspect the actual tax bite (the % of income paid in taxes) is much higher for the middle class than for the top 1%. If the top 1% bears 22% of the tax burden (see the chart in the article) then the next 19% bears 71% (though the two numbers — 90% and 22% are for different years)."

[14] Wolf, Martin (2014), "Wipe out rentiers with cheap money", *Financial Times* (May 6). Retrieved from http://www.ft.com/cms/s/0/d442112e-d161-11e3-bdbb-00144feabdc0. html#axzz31VJ8bWPs.

[15] Most observers wrongly assume that higher taxes and deferred debt have no impact on the new working class's long term behavior. The rising ranks of "disabled" and the shrinking labor force suggest that productive people do sense their deteriorating prospects and are responding "rationally".

[16] The IRS avoids verifying the assets of criminal, dangerous, sacrosanct (including those feigning disabilities) and well-connected elements who then become eligible for transfers.

[17] The first estate constituted 0.5% of France's population under the Ancien Régime; the second estate 2.5%. See Kingdom of France, Ancien Régime in France, *Wikipedia*.

[18] Novack, Jake (2014), "US seizing tax refunds of children over parents' debt?!" *CNBC* (April 11). Retrieved from http://www.cnbc.com/id/101576080#_gus. "For the past three years, the government has been confiscating hundreds of thousands of Americans' tax refunds, according to the Washington Post. It has already confiscated $1.9 billion in tax refunds this year alone. The amazing thing is that the government is doing this even if it has little or no proof and no exact details. And the letters the government sends to unsuspecting taxpayers are frightening, use accusatory language, and include other financial threats". However, the practice may soon cease. See Ohlemacher, Stephen (2014), "Social Security halts effort to

supposed to be equal, but some rich and poor animals are more equal than the drudges in new working class.[19]

Compression

The claim that the productive middle class is bearing the brunt of the new governance system is supported by the Economic Policy Institute (EPI) figures presented in Chapter 1. Real wages are declining absolutely and relative to corporate incomes. Professional salaries are being compressed. The labor force is shrinking. Young people are being harried into unpaid internships. The ranks of the disabled are swelling. Hidden inflation in medical,[20] education, housing and other government managed activities is eroding the middle class's purchasing power, at the same time the productive middle class is being forced to bear a greater and greater tax burden.

Politicians continually find it profitable to expand public services and transfers to big social advocacy and big business, funding these expenditures from the beleaguered new working class. The minimum wage for the new working class is sometimes raised, but it has fallen since 1968 in real terms and in the United States (US) is indexed to inflation in only 10 states. As transfers to the indigent increase, the attractiveness of productive labor diminishes, and with it the burden on those who continue to work. Likewise, large segments of the new working class seeing the deck stacked against them are reserving their effort and paring their ambitions. At the same time government regulations and taxes make it more and more difficult for small businesses to succeed. The result is a squeeze on the productive part of the population — more is required of it, and the incentives to work are lessened. Not surprising polls show that fewer and

---

collect old debts", *Yahoo Finance* (April 14). Retrieved from http://finance.yahoo.com/news/social-security-halts-effort-collect-old-debts-210451285--politics.html.

[19] Orwell, George (1945), *Animal Farm*, London: Secker and Warburg.

[20] The astronomical gaps between medical charges for standardized testing indicate the scale of hidden inflation. For example, see Kliff, Sarah (2014), "A $10,169 Blood Test is Everything Wrong with American Health care", *Vox*, August 16. "And that all makes it a bit baffling why, in California, a lipid panel can cost anywhere between $10 and $10,000. In either case, it is the exact same test." Retrieved from http://news.yahoo.com/10-169-blood-test-everything-170003116.html.

fewer Americans view themselves as middle class and are losing hope that they or their children can ascend the social ladder. 68% of respondents to a recent Federal Reserve study report that they are worse off or no better off than they were in 2008.[21] According to a Pew Research Center survey, just 44% of Americans believe they are part of the middle class,[22] and their aspirations have been correspondingly trimmed. In place of the familiar tripartite class structure: lower, middle and upper classes, the new structure is the entitled poor (some living quite well because of hidden incomes supplemented with transfers), the beleaguered new working class (most wage and salary workers), a struggling upper middle class ($200,000 adjusted gross income), and zillionaires.[23]

---

[21] "The Federal Reserve is telling us The Economy is Pitiful", *Huffintonpost*, August 7, 2014. Retrieved from http://www.huffingtonpost.com/2014/08/07/the-federal-reserve-think_n_5659224.html?ncid=txtlnkusaolp00000592#.

[22] Hughes, Deirdre (2014), "The middle class is a thing of the past", *Yahoo Finance* (April 4). Retrieved from http://finance.yahoo.com/blogs/hot-stock-minute/the-middle-class-is-a-thing-of-the-past-135730132.html. "That is the lowest level ever, down from 54% as recently as 2008. 40% identified themselves as lower-middle class or lower class in the January survey, compared to 25% in 2008. According to the definition offered up by the White House's 'Middle Class Task Force', the middle class in America is a thing of the past. How can that be? It is precisely because there is no empirical definition of what the middle class is or even a middle income range that defines the class. The fundamental principal that defines the American middle class is aspiration. The task force determined that: 'middle class families are defined more by their aspirations than their income'". "Based on that definition, the middle class is eroding simply because aspiration is eroding — and quickly. According to a Washington Post/Miller Center poll, just 39% of Americans believe their children will have a better standard of living than they do. A similar poll conducted by Gallup found the share of Americans who believe today's youth will have a better life than their parents has fallen sharply in recent years to 49% from 66% in 2008". "So, why has there been such a sharp decline in hope and aspiration?" Yahoo Finance Senior Columnist Michael Santoli believes income is the biggest factor. "Median wage in the country has not remotely kept pace with the expansion of the economy, even with inflation if you go back let's say 15 or 20 years". "The median income in the US as of 2012 was $51,017. That's down 10% from 1999 when the median income was $56,080, according to the Census Bureau".

[23] In America politicians protect themselves against compression by paying themselves salaries for life. The figures are $180,000 per year for the president, $174,000 per year for representatives and senators. They also receive supplementary pensions in the vicinity of $60,000 per year. Retrieved from http://www.ipl.org/div/farq/pensionFARQ.html.

New working class consumers both in America and the European Union (EU) find their purchasing power depleted by a variety of factors,[24] including rising multi-levy taxation,[25] $272 billion of healthcare fraud,[26] hidden inflation and fraud in education and healthcare, acknowledged inflation in the urban housing market,[27] and negligible interest on their savings. The result is tepid consumer demand that chills aggregate investment, but the politocrats do not care.[28] This plays into politicians' hands by providing a pretext for deficit spending to bolster consumer demand. One consequence is ever mounting national debt.[29] Easy mon-

---

[24] Bigot, Régis; Croutte, Patricia; Muller, Jörg and Osier, Guillaume (2012), "The Middle Classes in Europe: Evidence from the LIS Data", LIS Working Paper Series, Luxembourg Income Study (LIS), Asbl No. 580. Atkinson, Anthony B. and Brandolini, Andrea (2011), "On the identification of the 'middle class'", *ECINEQ WP 2011–217* (September). Retrieved from www.ecineq.org.

[25] For a contemporary Japanese example see "Japan's VAT Ratchet", *Wall Street Journal*, April 4, 2014. Retrieved from http://online.wsj.com/news/article_email/SB10001424052 702303978304579474922779106480-lMyQjAxMTA0MDAwNDEwNDQyWj.

[26] "Healthcare fraud in America, That's where the money is: How to hand over $272 billion a year to criminals", *Economist*, May 31, 2014. Retrieved from www.economist.com/node/21603026?fsrc=nlw|hig|29-05-2014|5356c958899249e1ccbfac7c|. "According to Donald Berwick, the ex-boss of Medicare and Medicaid (the public health schemes for the old and poor), America lost between $82 billion and $272 billion in 2011 to medical fraud and abuse".

[27] Goodkind, Nicole (2014), "More homes than ever are beyond the reach of the middle class, *Yahoo Finance!* (May 14). Retrieved from http://finance.yahoo.com/blogs/daily-ticker/more-homes-than-ever-are-beyond-the-reach-of-the-middle-class-150709372.html.

[28] Leightner, Jonathan (2014), *The Limits of Monetary, Fiscal, and Trade Policies: International Comparisons and a Solution*, Singapore: World Scientific Publishers. Wolf, Martin (2014), "Wipe out rentiers with cheap money", *Financial Times* (May 7) p. 9. "Cautious savers no longer serve a useful economic purpose ... Keynes even had a phrase for it — the 'euthanasia of the rentier ... There is a puzzle ... Why is private investment not stronger given that the non-financial corporate sector is apparently so profitable? ... What is needed ... are genuinely risk-taking investors. In their absence, governments need to use their balance sheets to build productive assets". The productive middle class and rentiers are not synonymous, but Keynesians often blur the distinction between productive people and the idle rich.

[29] There has been a concerted campaign to deny that excessive debt poses long risks to sustainable growth. The analysis is long on econometric correlation analysis with dubious

etary policy, ostensibly for the purpose of promoting effective demand, induces speculation and contributes directly to instability in financial markets.[30]

This is the dynamic process that escapes Summers and Krugman, and is denied by conservatives convinced that the middle class never had it so good.[31] They fail to recognize the government's squeezing of the new working class through excessive taxation, hidden inflation, asphyxiating regulations, mandates, executive orders, easy money, and

---

data, and short on commonsense. See Pescatoni, Andrea; Sandri, Damiano and John Simon, "Debt and Growth: Is There a Magic Threshold?" *IMF* (February 13). Clinch, Matt (2014), "IMF Paper Slams Reinhart–Rogoff", *Yahoo News* (February 14). Herndon, Thomas; Ash, Michael and Pollin, Robert (2013), "Does High Public Debt Consistently Stifle Economic Growth? A Critique of Reinhart and Rogoff", Political Economy Research Institute, Working Paper No. 322. Reinhart, Carmen, Reinhart, Vincent and Kenneth Rogoff (2012), "Public Debt Overhangs: Advanced-economy Episodes since 1800," *Journal of Economic Perspectives*, Vol. 25, No. 3, pp. 69–86.

[30] Johnson, Simon (2014), "Citigroup CEO Named to "Key Administration Post," *The Baseline Scenario* (April 1). Retrieved from http://baselinescenario.com/2014/04/01/citigroup-ceo-named-to-key-administration-post/. "The idea that Citigroup might now or soon have a viable 'living will' now seems preposterous. If top management cannot run sensible financial projections (that's the FED's view; see p. 7 of the full report), what is the chance that they can lay out a plausible plan to explain how the company, operating in more than 100 countries worldwide, could be wound down through bankruptcy — without any financial assistance from the government? According to the Dodd–Frank financial reform law, failure to submit a viable living will should result in remedial action by the authorities. Such action has now been taken: CEO Michael Corbat has been named to a top White House job, with responsibility for helping to develop 'financial capability for young Americans'". Cf. Johnson, Simon and Kwak, James (2013), *White House Burning: Our National Debt and What it Means to You*, New York NY: Vintage. Johnson, Simon and Kwak, James (2012), *13 Bankers: Wall Street Takeover and the Next Financial Meltdown*, New York NY: Vintage.

[31] Gilbert, Neil (2014), "The Denial of Middle-Class Prosperity Government data show that average disposable income has increased across all income groups since 1979", *Wall Street Journal* (May 16). "Countless reports now claim that the middle class is being crushed by inequality, declining mobility and diminishing income. A closer look at the facts suggests otherwise: Members of America's middle class are better off than they were 30 years ago, and they live much more comfortably than counterparts in other countries". The WSJ story disregards inflation and fails to focus on the productive middle class. Retrieved from http://online.wsj.com/news/article_email/SB10001424052702304893404579532302731093252-lMyQjAxMTA0MDEwNzExNDcyWj.

deficit spending is largely to blame for the secular stagnation they condemn and the crisis risk that they acknowledge.[32] Like Louis XVI they presume that fine tuning of current government policies is enough to assure better economic performance and sufficient well-being for a majority of the population, and like him too they are whistling past the graveyard.

---

[32] Schwartz, Nelson (2014), "The Middle Class is Steadily Eroding, Just Ask the Business World", *New York Times* (February 3). Retrieved from http://finance.yahoo.com/news/middle-class-steadily-eroding-just-013117051.html. "As politicians and pundits in Washington continue to spar over whether economic inequality is in fact deepening, in corporate America there really is no debate at all. The post-recession reality is that the customer base for businesses that appeal to the middle class is shrinking as the top tier pulls even further away". "More broadly, about 90% of the overall increase in inflation-adjusted consumption between 2009 and 2012 was generated by the top 20% of households in terms of income, according to the study, which was sponsored by the Institute for New Economic Thinking, a research group in New York". "Sears and J. C. Penney, retailers whose wares are aimed squarely at middle-class Americans, are both in dire straits. Last month, Sears said it would shutter its flagship store on State Street in downtown Chicago, and J. C. Penney announced the closings of 33 stores and 2,000 layoffs". According to Oxfam, while the recent financial crisis was an enormous burden on the world's poor, it ended up being a huge benefit to the rich elite. The very wealthiest people on earth collected 95% of the post-crisis growth in wealth". See Schofield, Matthew (2014), "Report: Richest 85 people own as Much as Half World's Globe's population, Oxfam reports", *Miami Herald* (January 20). Retrieved from http://www.miamiherald.com/2014/01/20/3882355/worlds-richest-85-people-have.html#storylink=cpy.

Chapter **5**

Liberalization for the Privileged

"At the dawn of a new year, the world is in the midst of several epic transitions. Economic growth patterns, the geopolitical landscape, the social contract that binds people together, and our planet's ecosystem are all undergoing radical, simultaneous transformations, generating anxiety and, in many places, turmoil. From an economic standpoint, we are entering an era of diminished expectations and increased uncertainty".

Klaus Schwab
Founder and Executive Chairman
World Economic Forum

A Good Start in the 1990s Gives Way to Disaster

The specter of secular stagnation, crisis, decay and discord is the result of a global double movement in the 1990s where insiders everywhere embraced a doublethink contradictory policy of economic liberalization and expanded government intervention designed to selectively garner the benefits of privatization, entrepreneurship and market competition for the establishment. The policy was a subterfuge. It was billed as Smithian (neoliberalism), but primarily benefited powerful insiders and big business.

The watchword of the double movement was globalization. The term among other things implied that nations were becoming more technologically, economically, socially, culturally and politically alike. Some claimed that all countries were destined to transition to post-industrial, democratic, progressive, equitable middle class societies with common living standards and policies. There would be an American or European Union (EU) dream at the rainbow's end for everyone.

From 1990 until 2008, it seemed as if the double movement would prove to be a winning strategy for the establishment and outsiders alike. The world economy grew well above the historical trend line driven by (1) China's and Vietnam's embrace of market communism, (2) market liberalization elsewhere in the less developed world including India and Brazil, and (3) American and EU economic expansion.[1] International trade surged, the debut of the euro generated heady expectations, and democracy seemed to be gaining worldwide momentum. The market was credited for this new found vitality and governments were applauded for unshackling the private sector. It was neoliberalism's euphoric moment: trade liberalization, business competition, increasing employment, low inflation and manageable fiscal deficits.

Few neoliberals appear to have anticipated that globalization might sour.[2] Most failed to recognize the reality of establishment domination in the west, and the danger of exporting the model to the east. Likewise, good times masked the limits of catch up growth in post-communist and post-socialist emerging nations,[3] and the spreading rot of regulatory creep, hidden inflation, stagnant wages, increasing inequality, deficit

---

[1] Maddison, Angus (2003), *The World Economy: Historical Statistics*, Paris: OECD. We asserted earlier that official data exaggerate real growth. Nonetheless, liberalization did visibly accelerate economic development in China, Vietnam, India and Brazil, and we accept official statistics are an indicator of improvement.

[2] The term transformation implies the shedding of one system and the creation of another. Transformations do not require specific outcomes. The term transition is commonly used to imply something more; that is, a transformation either to the American democratic free enterprise, or the European social democratic system. Globalizing systems change can be pernicious because it fails to clone either the America or European systems, or the western system they replicate is itself rotten.

[3] Rosefielde, Steven; Kuboniwa, Masaaki and Mizobata, Satoshi (2012), *Two Asias: The Growing Postcrises Divide*, Singapore: World Scientific.

spending, unrepayable indebtedness, and insider corruption in developing countries.[4]

Globalization has helped people to recognize that we are all in the same economic boat. But it is not the luxury liner that they expected. Instead of continuing to foster free markets, governments in nations across the planet are cloning each other's social rhetoric, regulatory, monetary and fiscal policies.[5] Establishments are making glowing promises funded by undeclared assaults on the new working class. Globalization has always offered mixed results — to many it is advantageous; to some it is damaging. Some gain new and cheaper products; others lose their jobs. But the balance is turning against most of us.

Post-Communist Modernization and Integration

The world brimmed with rival economic systems in 1985. The Soviet Union and its satellites, China, Vietnam, Laos, Cambodia and Cuba were authoritarian communist command regimes. For the most part they criminalized freehold property, markets and entrepreneurship (state ownership of the means of production, state monopoly of production and state control of new economic activities). Yugoslavia was an authoritarian labor managed market communist system, considered by

---

[4] Slowing economic growth in emerging countries is often described as the "middle income trap". Eichengreen, Barry; Park, Donghyun and Shin, Kwanho (2013), "Growth Slowdowns Redux: New Evidence on the Middle-Income Trap", NBER Working Paper No. 18673 (January). Retrieved from http://www.nber.org/papers/w18673. Aiyar, Shekhar; Duval, Romain; Puy, Damien; Wu, Yiqun and Zhang, Longmei (2013), "Growth Slowdowns ad the Middle-Income Trap", IMF Working Paper WP/13/71 (March). Retrieved from http://www.imf.org/external/pubs/ft/wp/2013/wp1371.pdf.

[5] "Larry Summers calls on US government to spend", *CNBC*, April 7, 2014. Retrieved from http://www.cnbc.com/id/101558487#_gus. "In the US the case for substantial investment promotion is overwhelming. Increased infrastructure spending would reduce burdens on future generations, not just by spurring growth but also by expanding the economy's capacity and reducing deferred maintenance obligations", he said. "In a globalized economy, the impact of these steps taken together is likely to be substantially greater than the sum of their individual impacts".

many at the time to be the wave of the future.[6] Western Europe was mostly social democratic and America by comparison was a democratic free enterprise system.[7] A large group of less developed countries relied on authoritarian state economic controls, capital restrictions and protectionism. International trade was encumbered.[8] There were some common values and sentiment favoring world government, but also ideological, cultural, and political discord symbolized by the cold war, and anti-colonial enmities.

The demise of Soviet communism and with it the temporary cessation of the cold war, together with China's and Vietnam's switch from command to market communism was advantageous to the world economy. These developments quickly opened previously closed economies to foreign direct investment, technology transfer and trade. Soon other protectionist emerging economies followed suit further strengthening the world economy.

Simultaneously, momentum began to build for something quite different from trade and competitive liberalization. Cross-border migration,[9] sundry forms of affirmative action, global integration, transnational organizations (EU, Association of Southeast Asian Nations (ASEAN), Trans Pacific Partnership (TPP)),[10] and expanded world government became part of the global agenda. The promise was diminished protectionism, enhanced global competition, prosperity, equity and social justice with a nascent common culture under the guidance of transnational institutions.

---

[6] Vanek, Jaroslav (1970), *The General Theory of Labor-Managed Market Economies*, Ithaca NY: Cornell University Press. Vanek, Jaroslav (1971), *The Participatory Economy. An Evolutionary Hypothesis and a Strategy for Development*, Ithaca NY: Cornell University Press.

[7] Macmillan, Harold (1939), *The Middle Way: A Study of the Problem of Economic and Social Progress In A Free and Democratic Society*, London: Macmillan. Giddens, Anthony (1998), *The Third Way: The Renewal of Social Democracy*, London: *Polity* and Giddens, Anthony (2000), *The Third Way and its Critics*, London: Polity.

[8] Williamson, John (1993), "Development and the 'Washington Consensus'", *World Development*, Vol. 21, pp. 1239–1336. Bhagwati, Jadish (2002), *Free Trade Today*, Princeton: Princeton University Press. Dollar, David and Kraay, Aart (2002), "Spreading the Wealth", *Foreign Affairs*, Vol. 81, No. January/February, pp. 120–133.

[9] OECD (2007), *Policy Coherence for Development* (2007): *Migration and Developing Countries*, OECD Development Centre, Paris: OECD.

[10] EU, Association of Southeast Asian Nations, and Trans Pacific Partnership.

This vision was and is attractive, but its fulfillment requires a significant restructuring of national and international economic systems and the creation of safeguards against their capture by establishment and private interests. Much of the economic restructuring happened; the safeguards did not. The result is that the promise of global liberalization has given way to a crisis-prone, economically stagnant, politically fragile new world order.[11]

Establishment Driven Globalization

Globalization since 1990 has been a mixed blessing with five primary features: market liberalization, internationalization, enhanced government economic power, insider enrichment, and the squeezing of the new working class. Generally, only the first two have been celebrated (market liberalization and internationalization). They offer substantial economic benefits to most of the world, and much has been gained. The other three features (state empowerment, insider capture and yoking the productive middle class) have been hidden in plain sight. In combination the three phenomena have undercut the promise of globalization and turned it into a curse.

Insiders have gained by altering the division of labor. Instead of pressing for the state as sole source provider of public programs and repressing market competition directly, they reengineered the economic mechanism by outsourcing and federalizing public programs, trafficking in state contracts, and peddling subsidies (tax preferences and regulatory favors),[12] including providing favors to monopolies and oligopolies at the expense of small family owned entrepreneurial business.[13] Simultaneously

---

[11] Thomas Piketty's proposal for a global wealth tax is a manifestation of the new one world movement. Piketty, Thomas (2014), *Capital in the Twenty-First Century*, Cambridge MA: Harvard University Press. Piketty recommends a global wealth tax to redress the planet's economic woes. Cf. Worstall, Tim (2014), "Why Thomas Piketty's Global Wealth Tax Won't Work", *Forbes* (March 30).

[12] Curry, William Sims (2014), *Government Abuse*, New Brunswick NJ: Transaction Press. "Government contracting is plagued by nefarious, amateurish, and criminal behavior. By awarding government contracts to corporations as compensation for lavish gifts and personal favors, the US government fails to serve the public interest effectively and honestly".

[13] Small entrepreneurial family businesses bear heavy inheritance tax burdens that force them out of business, and reduce competition. Insiders do not care much about small productive businesses that cannot afford to pay them tribute.

they have encouraged competition among domestic and foreign suppliers for their own benefit. This segmentation allows the establishment to exert market power as sellers, without ignoring the benefits of competition to them as buyers. The effort was win–win. It enabled insiders to eat a larger slice of a bigger cake by using market power to increase their revenues and competition to cut their costs, while posing as public benefactors.

The strategy also offered leverage. Insiders competed for greater wealth and power. They transformed themselves into global political entrepreneurs by gambling with public finance. They used state authority to excessively borrow and expand credit. They widened access to foreign markets, acquired foreign productivity enhancing technologies, and built international and transnational institutions to steer profits their way.

This is the new paradigm of national governance driving globalization. The main characteristic that distinguishes establishment regimes across the globe in this new paradigm is the scope of power sharing. Velvet demagogues like Vladimir Putin and Xi Jinping who hail from authoritarian traditions concentrate power narrowly within the inner circles of one-party states. Winner-take-all democracies like Thaksin Shinawatra's Thailand follow the same authoritarian script,[14] but the cast of players depends on electoral fortunes. Other regimes, especially those in politocratic America and Europe exhibit a mixed approach. The establishment has become an imperial caste that transcends party boundaries and the electoral cycle. Parties compete for voter favor and winners are advantaged, but the minority party often co-rules and shares the spoils.

---

[14] Race, Jeffrey (2014), "The Conflict in Thailand: Cultural Roots and the Middle Way Solution", *RSIS Commentaries*, No. 016/2014 (January 24). Retrieved from http://www.rsis. edu.sg/publications/Perspective/RSIS0162014.pdf?utm_source=getresponse&utm_ medium=email&utm_campaign=rsis_publications&utm_content=RSIS+Commentary+ 016%2F2014+The+Conflict+in+Thailand%3A+Cultural+Roots+and+The+Middle+Way+ Solution+by+Jeffrey+Race+%28Part+I0+. Race, Jeffrey (2014), "The Conflict in Thailand: Cultural Roots and the Middle Way Solution", *RSIS Commentaries*, No. 017/2014 (January 24). Retrieved from http://www.rsis.edu.sg/publications/Perspective/RSIS0172014. pdf?utm_source=getresponse&utm_medium=email&utm_campaign=rsis_publications& utm_content=RSIS+Commentary+017%2F2014+The+Conflict+in+Thailand%3A+ Conditions+for+a+Middle+Way+Solution+by+Jeffrey+Race+%28Part+II%29.

The approach provides continuity across electoral cycles and gives insiders an aura of democratic legitimacy.

The degree of establishment power sharing affects each system's economic growth potential. This partly explains why the Russian, Chinese, Thai, European and American regimes continue to perform diversely despite decades of globalization.[15] Establishment domination, the character of particular insiders, and their strategies of rule have partly countervailed the positive forces of foreign direct investment, technology transfer, cross border migration, and international trade.

Globalization's transformation of supply side aspects of the world economy in other words has not fulfilled advocates' dreams of liberty, equality, fraternity, social justice and affirmative action largely because establishments of various descriptions have been able to co-opt the new supply arrangements for their own purposes, making their regimes intrinsically anti-democratic. Globalization enabled them to bolster their power and wealth; not to maximize public well-being.

This double dynamic — insider capture of government resources and improved supply efficiency — has occurred in numerous countries. It can be more fully appreciated by reconsidering the experience in authoritarian states. The distinctive traits of the Soviet command model it will be recalled were the criminalization of private property, business and entrepreneurship. However, although these prohibitions were effective they did not always apply. The Soviet Union was not a comprehensively planned, market-free system as many supposed.[16] Informal market negotiations occurred between the state planning agency and the Communist Party leader; administrative department heads and "red directors" (factory managers), and enterprise bosses and workers. Dismantling administrative command planning therefore was a simple institutional matter, even though it was traumatic in practice.

Boris Yeltsin managed to discard command communism and switch to a new paradigm in 1992 with what seemed the whisk of a magic wand.[17]

---

[15] Ferguson, Niall (2008), *The Ascent of Money: A Financial History of the World*, New York NY: Penguin.

[16] Rosefielde, Steven (2007), *Russian Economy from Lenin to Putin*, New York NY: Wiley.

[17] Rosefielde, Steven and Dallago, Bruno (forthcoming), *Transformation and Crisis in Russia, Ukraine, Central and Eastern Europe: Challenges and Prospects*, London: Routledge.

He acted by privatizing enterprises, abolishing state price fixing, empowering managers to formally negotiate among themselves and with workers, and permitting managers to enter into outsourcing and other contractual relationships with the state. This reestablished the classical division between government and the private sector, but also entailed a regulatory overhaul. The state surrendered its right to command and control in exchange for the power to steer rents and market profits to insiders.

The entire government executive supply structure in Figure 3.1 was preserved, but the motivational mechanism changed by substituting rent-seeking and for-profit incentives for obedience (except in the military industrial complex and components of the energy sector).[18] Most of the regulatory institutions arrayed down the left hand column were retained, but their missions shifted. Instead of providing productive signals to red directors and workers by imposing mandates, requirements and rules; they became active instruments for indirectly granting rents. This is all that it took to replace Soviet state ownership and communist command with establishment economic management.

The transition from Mao Zedong's command regime to Dong Xiaoping's market communism system which preceded Russia's market transition was essentially the same, with three important qualifications.[19] First, China still criminalizes freehold property. From a legal point of view, all productive assets are leased by the state to Communist Party members and other citizens at the Party's discretion. Second, insider legitimacy and authority is dependent on the Communist Party, rather than the party depending on the man. In Russia the dependency is reversed. Putin is the source of all power; the majority United Russia Party (*Ediniya Rossiya*) is his servant. Third, China has chosen to become the industrial workshop of the world, and therefore has integrated itself into the global economy, whereas Russia remains mostly a protectionist natural resource hinterland.[20]

---

[18] The command principles and *khozraschyot* continues to apply in Figure 3.1, Ministry A, its departments and enterprises, but Ministry B has been deleted in favor of competitive enterprises.

[19] Rosefielde, Steven (2013), *Asian Economic Systems*, Singapore: World Scientific Publishers.

[20] World Bank, Country Partnership Strategy (CPS) for the Russian Federation, Report No. 65115-RU, November 2011. World Bank, Russia Economic Report, Confidence Crisis

Both nations rely heavily on the dark art of rent-granting; bestowing lucrative business favors by government leaders to lesser insiders in return for loyalty. China's approach is more dynamic, and its political regime more robust than Russia's, but it is also more combustible due to its insiders' propensity to leverage big speculative bets (e.g. in the current Chinese real estate bubble).[21] Russia's and China's productive middle classes (including peasants) have experienced some successes under the new paradigm, even allowing for doctored official statistics. However, the time seems to be nearing when insiders will begin tightening the screws on peasants, workers, professionals and small businesses.

The double movement in China and Russia — enhanced insider power and improved supply efficiency — was replicated in most emerging nations, and exhibits the same institutional changes. Property has been privatized in freehold or leasehold form; competition has been increased; labor protection has been reduced; and barriers to foreign investment have been pared. Meanwhile insiders have reinvented old institutions to serve themselves in new ways. Important details differ from country to country, but the trajectories are similar.

Globalization is homogenizing international production chains, national supply institutions, mechanisms and systems. It is expanding markets, competition and transnational networks, but the benefits are being narrowly channeled to national insiders and their allies. The transnational aspect of the process is epitomized by the EU.[22] Its member states have subordinated the high economic directorate of their own

---

"Exposes Economic Weaknesses", Report, March 31, 2014. Retrieved from http://www.worldbank.org/en/news/press-release/2014/03/26/russian-economic-report-31. The full report is retrieved from http://www.worldbank.org/content/dam/Worldbank/document/eca/RER-31-eng.pdf.

[21] Rapoza, Kenneth (2014), "When It Comes To Real Estate Bubbles, China's Got Nothing On Brazil", *Forbes* (January 18). Retrieved from http://www.forbes.com/sites/kenrapoza/2014/01/18/when-it-comes-to-real-estate-bubbles-chinas-got-nothing-on-brazil/.

[22] There are 17 members of the Eurozone: Austria, Belgium, Cyprus, Estonia, Finland, France, Germany, Greece, Ireland, Italy, Luxembourg, Malta, Netherlands, Portugal, Slovakia, Slovenia, and Spain. It is officially called the euro area, and is an economic and monetary union (EMU). Other EU states are obliged to join once they qualify, except the United Kingdom (UK) and Denmark. Monetary policy is the responsibility of the European Central Bank (ECB). Monaco, San Marino and Vatican City have concluded

national economies to the EU's supreme economic directorate (the European Commission) in many essential activities (Figure 3.1).[23] The European Commission has assumed exclusive supranational authority over: (1) the "customs union", (2) competition policy, (3) Eurozone (EZ) monetary power, (4) a common fisheries policy, (5) a common commercial policy, (6) conclusion of certain international agreements.

The European Commission also has the right to shared competence in (7) the internal market, (8) social policy for aspects defined in the treaty, (9) agriculture and fisheries, excluding the conservation of marine biological resources, (10) environment, (11) consumer protection, (12) transport, (13) trans-European networks, (14) energy, (15) the area of freedom, security and justice, (16) common safety concerns in public health aspects defined in the treaty, (17) research, development, technology and space, (18) development, cooperation and humanitarian aid, (19) coordination of economic and social policies, (20) common security and defense policies.

Additionally, the European Commission enjoys supporting competence in (21) protection and improvement of human health, (22) industry, (23) culture, (24) tourism, (25) education, youth sport and vocational training, (26) civil protection (disaster prevention), and (27) administration.

This has created an imperial caste of insiders who control the regulatory apparatus (including EU contracting) in the far left column of

---

formal agreements with the EU to use the euro. Andorra did so July 1, 2013. Kosovo and Montenegro have unilaterally adopted the euro, but are not EU members.

[23] The governing bodies of the EU's supranational governance tier are the European Parliament, Council of the EU, European Commission, the European Council, ECB, Court of Justice of the EU and European Court of Auditors. Competencies in scrutinizing and amending legislation are divided between the European Parliament and the Council of the EU while executive tasks are carried out by the European Commission and in a limited capacity by the European Council (not to be confused with the aforementioned Council of the EU). The monetary policy of the Eurozone is governed by the European Central Bank. The interpretation and the application of EU law and the treaties are ensured by the Court of Justice of the EU. The EU budget is scrutinized by the European Court of Auditors. There are also a number of ancillary bodies which advise the EU or operate in a specific area.

Figure 5.1 for their private benefit (often called the democratic deficit),[24] instead of the old Soviet-type ministerial plan command chains down the central column. Figure 5.1 has the same structure of Figure 3.1 and does double duty here illustrating the subtleties of the new global supply mechanism. The EU's imperial establishment is a formidable force, but still seeks more power by gradually acquiring taxing authority over EU member states and drawing the UK, Denmark and Sweden into the Eurozone.

America does not have an exact functional equivalent of the European Commission. The departments of the federal government's executive branch have similar powers, but there is no umbrella institution supervising departmental activities. American governmental department heads likewise have less clout because they must share insider power with a multitude of politicians at the federal level, whereas senior members of the European Commission only have to occasionally deal with the supranational heads of state in the Council of the EU and the European parliament.

This does not mean that America's politocrats distain channeling excess "liberalization" profits generated abroad through the aegis of transnational institutions to themselves. They are pressing for the development of a host of transnational entities including the Transatlantic Economic Council,[25] and Trans Pacific Trade Partnership in addition to existing international institutions like the International Monetary Fund (IMF) and

---

[24] Blokker, Paul (forthcoming), "The European Crisis as a Crisis of Democratic Capitalism", in Steven Rosefielde and Bruno Dallago, eds., *Transformation and Crisis in Russia, Ukraine, Central and Eastern Europe: Challenges and Prospects*, London: Routledge. Piattoni, Simona (2015), "Institutional Innovations and EU Legitimacy after the Crisis", in Steven Rosefielde and Bruno Dallago, eds., *Transformation and Crisis in Russia, Ukraine, Central and Eastern Europe: Challenges and Prospects*, London: Routledge.

[25] The Transatlantic Economic Council advances EU–US economic integration by bringing together governments, the business community, and consumers to work on areas where regulatory convergence and understanding can reap rewards on both sides of the Atlantic. Chaired by the EU Trade Commissioner and the US Deputy National Security Adviser for International Economic Affairs, the TEC provides a high-level forum to address complex areas like investment, financial markets, accounting standards, and secure trade, along with more technical issues. See Rosefielde, Steven (2013), "Assisting the EU: What America Ought to Do", Paper presented at the International Conference on Economic and Political Crises in Europe and the US: Prospects of Policy Cooperation, University of Trento.

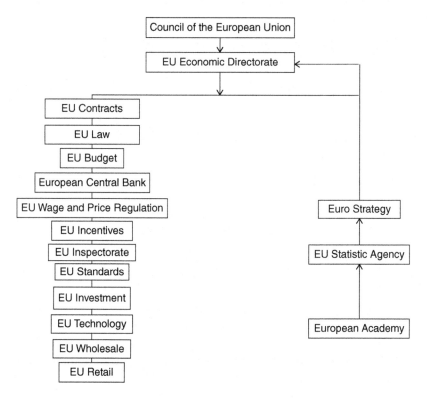

Figure 5.1.   EU supranational regulatory and rent granting apparatus.

World Bank to further these ambitions. If America's establishment somehow prevails, globalization will culminate in a supranationalized, and/or world government which almost exclusively benefits the highest ranking insiders.

Macroeconomic Policy

The Soviet supply system chart (Figure 3.1) lacked a macroeconomic policy component because comprehensive central planning made monetary and fiscal regulation superfluous.[26] Prices, wages, interest and foreign exchange

---

[26] This did not stop western Sovietologists from pretending that Soviet monetary and fiscal policy was somehow decisive. See Green, Donald and Higgins, Christopher (1977), *SOVMOD I: A Macroeconomic Model of the Soviet Union*, New York NY: Academic Press, Harcourt Brace and Jovanovich.

rates were fixed by the State Price Committee (Goskomtsen) and kept unchanged for decades, while fiscal policy was mostly an accounting matter because the state seldom borrowed significantly from itself. This changed in China, Russia and parts of the Third World in the late 1980s as markets started to play a significant role.

At first there was no clear pattern. Countries like Thailand, Indonesia, South Korea, the Philippines, and Hong Kong initially indulged in spending sprees and credit expansion, but after the 1997 Asian financial crisis adopted a more prudent approach emphasizing balanced budgets and slow monetary growth.

This new found prudence reflected the "New Keynesian" position that inflation and full employment were not substitutes, given sufficient wage flexibility and efficient markets. Unanticipated changes in productivity and therefore profits it was claimed caused business cycle oscillations and derivatively inflation and unemployment which lasted until price- and wage-setters disentangled real from nominal effects.[27] New Keynesians inferred from this that inflation was best addressed with monetary policy because the underlying problem was productivity driven changes in profitability, not shifts in consumer demand. Accordingly, central bankers were tasked with the mission of maintaining slow and stable inflation sufficient to assure full employment. Although, central bankers were supposed to be less concerned with real economic activity than with inflation, many came to believe that full employment and 2% inflation could be sustained indefinitely by what some labeled "divine coincidence".[28]

This miracle was said to be made all the better by the discovery that real economic performance could be regulated with a single monetary instrument, the short term interest rate. Happily, arbitrage (competitive adjust of interest rates factoring in different degrees of risk) across time meant that central bankers could control all temporal interest rates. Arbitrage across asset classes implied that the United States (US) Federal

---

[27] Lucas, Robert Jr. (1972), "Expectations and the Neutrality of Money", *Journal of Economic Theory*, Vol. 4, No. 2, pp. 103–124. Kydland, Phil and Prescott, Edward (1982), "Time to Build and Aggregate Fluctuations", *Econometrica*, Vol. 50, No. 6, pp. 1345–1370.

[28] Blanchard, Oliver and Gali, Jordi (2007), Real Wage Rigidities and the New Keynesian Model, *Journal of Money, Credit, and Banking*, Vol. 39, No. 1, pp. 25–65.

Reserve could similarly influence risk adjusted rates for diverse securities. Fiscal policy, which had ruled the roost under the influence of orthodox Keynesianism from 1950–1980 in this way, was relegated to a subsidiary role aided by theorists' beliefs in the empirical validity of the argument that changes in government spending were reciprocally offset in the private sector (Ricardian equivalence arguments), and skepticism about lags and political priorities.[29]

Monetarists made some minor concessions to fiscal policy advocates, recognizing that miracles might not last forever. The consensus view held that automatic stabilizers like unemployment insurance should be retained to share risks in case there were any unpredictable shocks. Commercial bank credit similarly continued to be regulated, and federal deposit insurance preserved to deter bank runs, but otherwise finance was lightly supervised; especially "shadow banks", hedge funds and derivatives. This view of the reasons for deregulation of the financial sector was popularized by Federal Reserve System (FED) Chairman Alan Greenspan.

New Keynesian advocates thus insisted that America and nations across the globe could enjoy reasonable economic growth with low deficit spending, moderate national debt and a monetary policy targeted to achieve a 2% rate of inflation. There was no place for Summers and Krugman's concern about economic stagnation in this conception. Extravagant credit and money creation needlessly entailed grave inflationary risk, and deficit spending served no constructive purpose.

The establishment was content with New Keynesian doctrine until the 2008 global financial crisis because insiders were prospering without resorting to currency debasement and prodigal deficit spending. They oversaw the step by step dismantling of Franklin Roosevelt's New Deal anti-monopoly and financial regulations, while simultaneously fanning speculative flames by energetically promoting subprime mortgages. Profits soared on Wall Street and speculative windfalls abounded without igniting inflation in other sectors or accelerating deficit spending and debt accumulation. These easy gains were supplemented by captured benefits from rapid economic development in emerging nations and

---

[29] See Grauwe, Paul De (2010), "Top-Down versus Bottom-Up Macroeconomics", *CESifo Economic Studies*, Vol. 56, No. 4, pp. 465–497.

profits from hidden inflation in housing, education, healthcare and environmental programs.[30]

The 2008 financial crisis brought the divine coincidence era to a screeching halt. Ben Bernanke Chairman of the FED and fiscal authorities in America and Europe responded to a wave of cascading financial bankruptcies and plummeting demand with emergency money and credit expansion, massive deficit spending and financial rescue packages. The infusions were supposed to be temporary. Once confidence was restored, macroeconomic theorists expected divine coincidence policy to be restored. But the expectation was derailed by the opportunities for personal benefit offered the establishment in the new situation. The lucrative possibilities of permanently combining financial liberalization with extravagant easy money policies and deficit spending increased insider ambitions.[31] Fears of hyperinflation lost their urgency and the

---

[30] Rosefielde, Steven and Razin, Assaf (2012), "The 2008–2009 Global Crisis", in Steven Rosefielde, Masaaki Kuboniwa and Satoshi Mizobata, eds., *Prevention and Crisis Management: Lessons for Asia from the 2008 Crisis*, Singapore: World Scientific.

[31] Pollock, Alex (2014), "Fannie and Freddie are obviously SIFIs", *AEI* (April 22). Retrieved from http://www.aei.org/article/economics/financial-services/housing-finance/fan-and-fred-are-obviously-sifis/?utm_source=today&utm_medium=paramount&utm_campaign=042214. "Consider size. Fannie's total assets are bigger than JPMorgan Chase and Bank of America, and Fannie and Freddie are each bigger than Citigroup, Wells Fargo, Goldman Sachs, Morgan Stanley, Prudential, and AIG, not to mention many others. Fannie's $3.3 trillion in assets would make it the No. 1 SIFI of all, while Freddie's $2 trillion would rank No. 4.

In addition to their massive size, Fannie and Freddie sport extreme leverage. Fannie is leveraged 341:1 and has a leverage capital ratio of a risible 0.29%. Similarly, Freddie has leverage of 153:1 and a leverage capital of an almost as risible 0.65%.

Leveraged real estate has a long and painful record of being at the center of many banking collapses and financial crises, as yet once again in 2007–2009. Fannie and Freddie represent about 60% of the credit risk of the huge American housing finance market, making them by far the largest concentration of leveraged credit and house price risk in the world.

More than $5 trillion of the obligations of these hyper-leveraged institutions are widely held throughout the US financial system and around the world by banks, central banks, other official bodies and many other investors. This includes over $1 trillion of Fannie and Freddie obligations bought by the Federal Reserve Banks".

pretense of deficit cutting faded.[32] Politicians today are prepared to live with permanent excess money creation (albeit with some "tapering" from current rates) and deficit spending if it pays sufficient insider dividends. Countries across the globe from Japan to Argentina have joined the party.[33] The credo today and for tomorrow is that if establishments win, anything goes.[34]

Establishment Globalization

The challenged posed by secular stagnation, crises, decay and discord today cannot be adequately understood in traditional terms. The main driver as shown above is not business mania, or as Marxists claim, the contradictions of capitalism. It is insider globalization; that is, the worldwide quest by national establishments and their various allies to maximize rewards for themselves derived by government programs, corruption,[35]

---

[32] Hook, Janet (2014), "Senate Approves Suspension of US Debt Ceiling: Bill Suspends Cap on Government Borrowing Through March 2015", *Wall Street Journal* (February 14). Retrieved from http://online.wsj.com/news/articles/SB1000142405270230370430457937914 0420941048?mg=reno64-wsj&url=http%3A%2F%2Fonline.wsj.com%2Farticle%2 FSB10001424052702303704304579379140420941048.html. Kessler, Glen (2014), "Is Suspending the Debt Limit a 'Blank Check' for Obama?" *Washington Post* (February 19). Retrieved from ogs/fact-checker/wp/2014/02/19/is-suspending-the-debt-limit-a-blank-check-for-obama/?tid=hpModule_f8335a3c-868c-11e2-9d71-f0feafdd1394.

[33] Taylor, Paul (2014), "'Great Stretch' to secure Greek debt return", *Reuters* (April 13). Retrieved from http://finance.yahoo.com/news/great-stretch-secure-greek-debt-075544601.html. "It is a government version of the 'extend and pretend' behavior of private lenders who keep bad loans on their books, hoping something will turn up, rather than writing down losses".

[34] Williams, Pete (2014), "Supreme Court Strikes Down Another Limit on Money in Politics", *NBC News* (April 2). Retrieved from http://www.nbcnews.com/politics/supreme-court/supreme-court-strikes-down-another-limit-money-politics-n69681.

[35] Dahlburg, John-Thor (2014), "Corruption Costing Bloc $162 Billion Annually", *AP* (February 3). Retrieved from http://news.yahoo.com/eu-corruption-costing-bloc-162-billion-annually-114132882.html. "Corruption affects all member countries of the EU and costs the bloc's economies around €120 billion ($162.19 billion) a year, an official EU report published Monday said".

self-serving regulation, over-taxation, fiscal leverage, credit expansion, liberalization, supranationalization and world government.[36]

This means that the solution does not lie just in better regulating the private sector, or devising superior microeconomic and macroeconomic policies, but in clipping the establishment's wings.[37] The world will not be spared from secular stagnation, crises, decay and discord, and the global new working class's plight alleviated unless insiders are defanged.

---

[36]"A Bipartisan Taxpayer Raid: The Farm Bill is the Real Reason Members were Cheering Tuesday Night", *Wall Street Journal*, January 28, 2014. Retrieved from http://online.wsj.com/news/article_email/SB10001424052702304007504579349183643865294-lMyQjAx MTA0MDIwOTEyNDkyWj. "The real headline is how complete a victory this is for the entitlement and farm-subsidy *status quo*". "The farm crew is also boasting they eliminated the 'direct payment' program — handouts that go to growers whether they produce a crop or not. Yet the $5 billion in savings is rolled back into the government-subsidized (and uncapped) crop-insurance program as well as a new 'shallow-loss' program that guarantees farmers' revenues and could balloon to $14 billion a year".

[37]Vaishnav, Milan (2014), "Crime but no punishment in Indian Elections", *Carnegie Endowment for International Peace* (January 24). Retrieved from http://carnegieen dowment.org/2014/01/24/crime-but-no-punishment-in-indian-elections/gz9k. "Consider this extraordinary figure: 30% of members of parliament have criminal cases pending against them. And that is an increase from the previous election in 2004, when "only" 24% of MPs were similarly situated".

Race, Jeffrey (2014), "The Conflict in Thailand: Cultural Roots and the Middle Way Solution", *RSIS Commentaries*, No. 016/2014 (January 24). Retrieved from http://www.rsis.edu.sg/publications/Perspective/RSIS0162014.pdf?utm_source=getresponse&utm_medium=email&utm_campaign=rsis_publications&utm_content=RSIS+Commentary+0 16%2F2014+The+Conflict+in+Thailand%3A+Cultural+Roots+and+The+Middle+Way +Solution+by+Jeffrey+Race+%28Part+I0+.

Chapter 6

East-West Polarization

The term globalization in popular parlance implies the creation of a new world order where national rivalries are subordinated to the higher values of efficiency, productivity and prosperity. All nations are supposed to embrace universal values, shun polarization and support the inviolability of post-war territorial boundaries. Supranationality is acceptable; conquest and absorption are not.

The dream has never been realistic,[1] but appeared to be almost true while Russia, China, India and parts of the Islamic world embraced aspects of liberalization to spur domestic economic growth and catch up, biding their time until they could challenge western hegemony. The financial crisis of 2008, contemporary western secular stagnation, and entitlement politics have pushed Russia and China's long term authoritarian agendas forward. They discovered that the west in its current form is a "paper tiger" that cannot maintain its economic superiority or nimbly redeploy resources to external challenges. America (US) and the European Union (EU) refuse to accept their weakness and reform themselves, and in any event lack the political will to parry Russia's and China's arms buildups.

---

[1] Mills, Quinn and Rosefielde, Steven (2009), *Rising Nations: What America Should Do*, New York NY: Amazon.

Russia's annexation of Crimea and China's assertive territorial claims in the China Sea in 2014 largely reflect the new problematic.[2] Both emergent superpowers today cannot be to be restrained by western rules and reject the west's entitlement culture. They believe that they can have their cake and eat it. This means that they can carry on business as usual with US and the EU after economic sanctions fatigue depletes the west's resolve, while simultaneously prevailing in east–west turf wars. They are convinced that western countermeasures will be blunted by the EU's dependence on Russian natural resources, America's and Europe's reliance on low cost Chinese outsourcing and balance of payments deficit financing.[3] Russia and China are full-fledged members of the World Trade Organization, making it difficult for the west to bar their market access. Washington sometimes hints that it can discipline Russia and China by curtailing technology transfers, but is unlikely to do it. Russia and China consequently have a golden opportunity to bend the global power balance their way with multiple instruments including military force, subversion, intimidation, market power and "enlightened conservative" authoritarian ideologies.

Their authoritarianism is a handicap, but does not preclude the east's success. Few countries will be lured by the appeal of Russian and Chinese law and order, nationalism, populism, superpower or even rapid growth driven prosperity. However, Moscow and Beijing may have little difficulty building their domestic authority on national pride, duty, civic virtue, military power, and dynamism that eastern leaders contrast with the western decadence and decline. Globalization on western terms is dead; slain by repolarization.

The resulting struggle for hegemony will exacerbate the gathering economic storm. The west's diminishing economic power vis-à-vis the

---

[2] Anh, Mguyen Thi Lan (2014), "*Xisha (Paracel) Islands: A Rejoinder*", *RSIS Commentaries*, No. 117/2014 (June 20). "Purely based on the application of international law of the sea, and notwithstanding the sovereignty dispute over the Paracels, the Haiyang Shiyou 981 oil rig was transported by China recently to a location deep inside the EEZ and continental shelf of Vietnam".

[3] The US federal government owes Russia $1.6 billion and China $1.3 trillion. Roos, Dave; Conger, Cristen and Clifton, Jacob (2013), "Top 10 Countries the U.S. Owes Money To". Retrieved from http://people.howstuffworks.com/5-united-states-debt-holders.htm#page=0. The figures are for 2013.

east will depress its growth potential, increase financial and speculative risk, aggravate the battle for domestic resources, augment the productive middle class's burden and heighten international insecurities. The countermeasures that will be adopted by America and the EU cannot be precisely predicted. However, it is a foregone conclusion that Russia's and China's military challenge will rapidly mount in the next *quinquennium* without any effective western response. China's defense spending has been growing at double digit rates for decades while western defense expenditures have sharply declined,[4] and the dollar value of China's weapons procurement exceeds America's, although this is hidden by the Central Intelligence Agency (CIA's) manipulation of purchasing power parities, and other improper adjusted factor costing techniques.[5] Russia weapons production fell 90% after the Soviet Union collapsed in 1991, but has recovered much of the lost ground. Current procurement levels properly computed probably exceed America's.[6]

Russia and China unlike their western adversaries are not paper tigers. Their authoritarian cultures allow them to devote immense shares of their gross domestic product (GDP) to defense. When the west is strong, these outlays are mostly wasteful. However, when the west is weak and inert, Moscow and Beijing can reap substantial militarization dividends at the expense of the west and global stability.

---

[4] *Military and Security Developments Involving the People's Republic of China* (2013), Annual Report to Congress, Office of the Secretary of Defense. Retrieved from http://www.defense.gov/pubs/2013_china_report_final.pdf.

[5] Rosefielde, Steven (2012), "Economics of the Military-Industrial Complex", in Michael Alexeev and Shlomo Weber, eds., *The Oxford Handbook of Russian Economy*, Oxford: Oxford University Press. Rosefielde, Steven (1987), *False Science: Underestimating the Soviet Arms Buildup*, Rutgers NJ: Transactions. Rosefielde, Steven (2005), *Russia in the 21ˢᵗ Century: Prodigal Superpower*, Cambridge: Cambridge University Press.

[6] Rosefielde, Steven (2013), "Russian Economic Reform 2012: "Déjà vu All Over Again", in Stephen Blank, ed., *Politics and Economics in Putin's Russia*, Carlisle Barracks: Strategic Studies Institute and US Army War College. Rosefielde, Steven (forthcoming), *The Kremlin Strikes Back: Russia and the West after Crimea's Annexation*, Cambridge: Cambridge University Press.

Chapter 7

Degeneration, Crisis and Disorder

The global economy experienced a sustained advance after World War II due to technological progress, modernization, development, marketization, liberalization, democratization, globalization, the demise of communist command planning and the end of the Cold War. Success however often sows the seeds of decay. The world economy after a good start appears to have lost its vitality during the 2008 global financial crisis.

The causes of this dyspepsia are self-apparent: government and business corruption, executive orders, legislative mandates, over-regulation, over-taxation of the productive middle class, abusive entitlements, excessive national indebtedness and state abetted speculation. The malaise is now fashionably called secular stagnation. The term is helpful, but incomplete because it implies crisis free stability of three sorts. First, it suggests a steady state without winners and losers. This is misleading. Although, per capita gross domestic product (GDP) is growing at a snail's pace or worse (adjusted for hidden inflation), politarchs and their entitled beneficiaries (rich and poor), financial speculators and wealthy investors are flourishing at the expense of the productive middle class (workers). Middle class workers are experiencing job losses, diminishing real wages, increased multi-source taxation, zero interest on savings and galloping hidden inflation in educational, medical and other services. The aggregate stability conceals a cauldron of stress and discontent. Second, the global economy is overdosing on monetary and fiscal stimulus. There will be a day of reckoning. In economics, as in physics mortals cannot defy the law of gravity and the mega stimulus sustaining secular stagnation will end badly, even if catastrophe is somehow averted by releasing pressure through rampant inflation and investor haircuts.

Secular stagnation is misleading in a third sense. It implies social and political stability. Reality is just the reverse. Not only is the productive middle class becoming increasing restive,[1] but nothing placates the

---

[1] Newman Rick (2014), "Americans are down on America", *Yahoo Finance* (July 6). Retrieved from http://finance.yahoo.com/news/americans-are-down-on-america-190304928.html. "We are No. 33! That is the bottom line in a new Gallup poll measuring the extent of freedom in 135 countries. Only 79% of Americans say they are satisfied with their freedom to choose what to do with their lives, down from 87% in 2008. The top five nations where people feel most satisfied with their freedoms are New Zealand, Australia, Cambodia, Sweden and the United Arab Emirates (UAE). At No. 33, the US is sandwiched between Bahrain and Cameroon.

The US is one of the few places where freedoms appear to be on the wane.

That new-found humility corresponds with an economic comedown that is looking permanent for an uncomfortably large portion of Americans. The recession that ended in 2009 ravaged the economic fortunes of many American families, with median household wealth still about 40% lower than it was before the recession. Jobs have finally started to return, but for many workers, pay is lower than it used to be. People feel they are falling behind, and the data show they are not imagining things. That is a loss of economic freedom, which impacts other choices.

Many Americans seem to question the basic premise that everybody can get ahead in the so-called land of the free. A recent analysis by US today found living the American Dream, loosely defined, costs a typical family of four roughly $130,000 per year. That is in a country where the median household income is only about $53,000, or less than half of what is needed for a middle-class lifestyle".

Such tangible declines in middle-class living standards represent the most important economic trend in a generation. The recovery that followed the recession and began in 2009 has been the weakest since the 1930s. A gridlocked Washington may deserve some of the blame, yet digital technology and globalization have allowed companies to locate work wherever it is cheapest and replace employees with computers, robots and other gizmos. Americans are rightly fed up with their government but there may not be all that much Washington can do to reinvigorate an economy that still has too much debt clogging its veins.

entitlement crowd (including politarchs, insiders, Wall Street and big social advocacy). As soon as the powerful receive unmerited transfers, they up the ante with fresh demands at the expense of productive middle class workers. The result is acrimonious political and social cultures of grievance and discontent that are becoming increasingly combustible. Global economic turmoil is not just about vanished prosperity and financial crises; it is about political and social strife (*omni bellum contra omnes*).[2]

Finally, secular stagnation erroneously suggests a stable geopolitical order where everyone accedes to *pax occidentalis* (peace on the west's terms). While it appears that most nations were prepared to embrace the west's rules for globalization before 2008, it has recently become self-evident that Russia, China and many countries in the Middle East are no longer on board. Recognizing that the west is on the ropes, and too corrupt to heal itself Russia, China and Islamic State of Iraq and Levant (ISIS) can be expected to constantly press the boundaries of toleration with military force, subversion, financial pressure and other exertions of economic power. This means that due to secular stagnation, financial crises, and social turmoil, the west will find itself harried by foreign badgering.

The gathering storm appears to be a Category 5 hurricane. Can it be averted, and if not, what will be the consequences? We are not economic or historical determinists. The accumulating evidence appears to indicate that the world will suffer grievously, but the details will only become clear in the fullness of time. Most of the pain still can be avoided. The antidotes are obvious. Eradicate government and business corruption. Curtail executive orders and legislative mandates. Abolish over-regulation and over-taxation of the productive middle class. Eliminate pro-insider regulations. Terminate abusive entitlements, excessive national and private indebtedness, and state abetted speculation. Downsize bloated government by eliminating insider programs and providing basic services only when the state has a competitive advantage over private outsourcers. Build credible deterrents against foreign aggressors, and shun transgressions against others.

---

[2] Hobbes, Thomas (1651), *Leviathan*, Oxford: Clarendon Press.

These policies are not difficult to craft, but they require goodwill and sacrifice. This is the rub, not neoclassical microeconomic and macro-economics technicalities. The Category 5 hurricane can be averted, but economics and politician must cease hiding behind conceptual blinders and do the right thing, instead of indulging themselves in vicious circles.[3] The urgent need is for deeds, not words.

---

[3] Carly Fiorina, interview on Bloomberg TV, June 25, 2014, 8 AM. Carly Fiorina, formerly CEO of HP chairs the board of a non-profit which is the largest micro-lender, some $6 billion in loans averaging $150 per loan; 93% of the loans are to women to finance business or professional efforts. She was asked rhetorically, "Is there anything going on in Washington to help people lift themselves out of poverty?" She answered, "No. In fact, everything done there makes it more difficult". She was referring to all the rules and regulations about businesses and employment and tax-related reporting.

Part II
Obstacles to Crisis Prevention

Chapter **8**

Words Instead of Action

Stagnation of the world economy and resultant financial and economic crises can be avoided, but the insiders who control the world's governments fail to take the necessary actions. They fail to do so because they are profiting personally from the imperfections in the current system, do not hesitate to lie, are derelict in their duty, and lack the resolve to see beyond the tip of their noses.[1] They are willfully ignorant in the root sense they ignore what they don't want to see, creating a governmental age of ignorance.[2] This chapter shows that the behavior of insiders toward the problems of the global economy mirrors their behavior toward other problems of public

---

[1] Carter, Zach (2014), "Barney Frank 'Appalled' By Obama Administration: 'They Just Lied To People'", *Huffington Post* (August 1). Retrieved from http://www.huffingtonpost. com/2014/08/01/barney-frank-obama-lie_n_5642132.html?ncid=txtlnkusaolp00000592#. "The rollout was so bad, and I was appalled — I do not understand how the president could have sat there and not been checking on that on a weekly basis", Frank told HuffPost during a July interview. "But frankly, he should never have said as much as he did, that if you like your current healthcare plan, you can keep it. That was not true. And you should not lie to people. And they just lied to people". Conover, Christopher J. (2014), "Jonathan Gruber: The $6 Million Stonewaller", *Forbes*, December 11. Retrieved from http://www.aei.org/ publication/jonathan-gruber-6-million-stonewaller/?utm_source=today&utm_medium=paramount&utm_campaign=121214.

[2] Willful ignorance is easily concealed behind a welter of extraneous information. See Hall, Crystal, Ariss, Lynn and Todorov, Alexander (2007), "The Illusion of Knowledge: When More Information Reduces Accuracy and Increases Confidence," *Organizational Behavior and Human Decision Processes*, Vol. 103, pp. 277–290.

concern including poverty, climate change, health care, and needed national economic transitions.

Insiders Enrich Themselves while Economic Growth Slows and Financial Crises Loom

Each nation operates in much the same way. The governing insiders — politarchs in America and EU or their more authoritarian counterparts elsewhere — identify public needs and promise to satisfy them. The insiders propose programs to meet the needs. The programs are implemented at high cost. Insiders benefit in a variety of ways from the programs. The public needs are not satisfied; public problems are not solved; but insiders have benefited. Failures, which are continual, are blamed on political opponents. In a Western democracy the political opponents are sometimes able by election to seize power and resume the process of promises and failure in order to benefit themselves. In Russia, political opponents are blamed and harassed. What is common to sovereign democracies in the West and in Russia is that public problems are not resolved despite much money and other resources being devoted to the effort. In China there is no pretense of democracy, so that China is not now a sovereign democracy. Nonetheless the Chinese authoritarian government claims popular support for itself and justifies this by the economic progress being made. Even in China there is the same process: promises to alleviate public problems; expensive programs from which insiders benefit, and public problems at best remedied a bit but left largely unsolved. This has become a world-wide dynamic — one in which insiders enrich themselves all the while offering empty promises to help others. This is an underlying reason why economic growth is slowing internationally and why additional financial crises are certain to occur.

Failure of Government Spending to Achieve Announced Purposes

Failure to end poverty in America

The poor play a special role in the politics of most countries today. It is not that they are helped very much. Nor is it that they have much prospect of greatly improving their living standards. But they play a very significant public role for the insiders who run today's governments.

In almost all the world today there is no source of political legitimacy except the will of the people. In democracies legitimacy is granted to the government via elections; in authoritarian states legitimacy is granted to the government by what are claimed to be expressions of the people's satisfaction. Since most people in all societies are not wealthy, it is common for governments of all sorts to declare their commitment to the advancement of the poor.

In the developed countries great sums are spent for the purpose of ameliorating poverty. Many programs consume the attention of many bureaucrats. In the United States in the 1960s a war was declared on poverty by the then President Lyndon Johnson. The stated purpose was to eliminate poverty in America over a period of a few years.

It is now some 50 years after the war on poverty was launched in America. The official statistics about poverty in America show 22.4% of the American population in poverty in 1959, just before the advent of the war on poverty. The low point in the official statistics was the year 1973 at 11.1%. This was within a decade after the war on poverty began. The most recent statistics are for 2012 when the rate was 15%.

Accepting official statistics which may be biased in various ways, we still are entitled to ask: What happened 40 years ago (after 1973) to stop progress against ending poverty in America? The economy, measured by official statistics, has grown since the 1970s, including on a per capita basis. A great deal of money has been spent alleviating poverty.

The answer is that poverty in America remains real; the commitment to solutions is not. Insiders have co-opted the issue for their own benefit. If poverty were seriously addressed the cost of eradicating it would be greater than politicians are willing to pay. If it were eliminated, politocrats would lose significant opportunities for personal enrichment. This pattern is repeated continually in social concerns related to poverty including crime, education, and housing.

The failure of the American war on poverty has now continued for four decades. Insiders insist that the failure is due to a weak economy (though in other contexts they stress the strength of the economy under their supervision), and to bureaucratic inertia. It is therefore a failure of the system, in their representation, rather than of themselves.

Anti-poverty programs are a rich source of gain for insiders and their supporters. Recently in America the majority of people relying on food stamps (a major American anti-poverty program) are of working age, not children or the elderly. Some 15% of the entire population now receives food stamps. The very poor receive little. The cash allowance per meal per person seems to be about $1.40. This is not generous at all. But many people who receive food stamps spend the money on non-essentials like junk food and luxury items — presumably because they do not need money for basics.[3] It appears that stamps are channeled to supporters of political figures. These things are reported continually in the local media of American states and cities.

It is revealing how the politarchy has dealt in recent decades with America's poor. An especially instructive example involves the subprime mortgage episode. In a nutshell, the government sponsored mortgage lending to low-income people in order that they would have housing, despite many of these people being unable to pay their mortgage bills. In the process financial companies speculated in the mortgages. From this the financial crisis of 2007–2008 originated.[4] When the financial crisis came, many people were evicted from their homes since they could not pay their mortgages. Another government program ostensibly to help people retain their homes benefited primarily the banks. Over a period of a few years the government drove millions out of their homes while financial firms benefited greatly.[5] A recent study has documented the very severe impact of losing one's home on the poor.[6] That some of the financial firms involved collapsed in the financial crisis does not change the net assessment. The politicians who sponsored the impoverishment of the poor and who always professed exactly the opposite purpose were reelected and later retired from office undefeated. It is hard to view their record as anything but duplicity, although they blame anyone they can.

The American war on poverty has been a colossal failure for poor; it has been a great success for the insiders. For the insiders it is a gift that keeps on giving. Every Administration proposes new programs to combat

---

[3] http://www.fns.usda.gov/snap/eligible-food-items.

[4] Rosefielde, Steven and Mills, Quinn (2013), *Democracy and its Elected Enemies*, Cambridge: Cambridge University Press.

[5] *Ibid.*

[6] Gudrais, Elizabeth (2014), "Disrupted Lives: Sociologist Matthew Desmond Details the Devastating Effects of Eviction on America's Poor", *Harvard Magazine*, (January–February), Vol. 116, No. 3, pp. 38–43.

poverty.[7] The taxpayers pay for this, funneling money into the pockets of the politarchy. This is the classic behavior of insider government in our time.

Some Success in the Third World

Still, in developing countries extreme poverty — people living on a dollar a day, for example — has been considerably reduced over the past few decades. It is not clear today that this process is continuing. Nor is the level of living considerably better than abject poverty. During the same period, however, it is certain that insiders have greatly benefited and continue to benefit today.

Even where a country achieves substantial economic growth the poor may not be helped. In developed economies economic growth must be of the right sort to assist the poor. If growth is more production without employment growth, then whether or not poverty is alleviated depends entirely on the distribution of the additional growth. If the additional economic growth is merely more bureaucratic wheel-spinning, then even distribution to the poor may not be helpful in alleviating poverty. If growth is accompanied by pollution and environmental damage, then the poor may be worse off because damage to health and living conditions, even if there are some additional jobs created. If economic growth is to lessen poverty, it must create jobs that are taken by the poor; the jobs must have adequate compensation; the living conditions of the poor must be improved, not worsened; and the distribution of gains from economic growth must include the poor.

In developing countries economic growth generally leaves a residue of poor in the traditional sectors of the economy — often primarily in agriculture. Often, also, jobs in the modern sector are not sufficient to allow people to escape from poverty.

For the poor to benefit from economic growth, growth must be of the right type in both developed and developing countries. This is a responsibility of the government and private business people — that is, of insiders. But in their haste to enrich themselves, insiders rarely display concern for the poor — who therefore remain poor.

---

[7] Rampton, Roberta (2014), "Obama Targets Poverty in San Antonio, Philadelphia and Other U.S. 'Zones.'" *Reuters* (January 8).

Enriching the Wealthy

As the distribution of income has become more unequal in the world, politicians have found it useful to promise to reverse the process.

But there is no evidence that a reversal is occurring. Quite the contrary, the concentration of wealth continues.

What is now beginning is a series of government programs that will be directed at decreasing the income gap. They will involve education, job training, savings incentives, etc. The programs are certain to enrich insiders who will benefit in many ways. They are not likely to do much for the poor.

In this regard politicians today are disciples of Joseph Goebbels — they are masters of saying one thing and doing the opposite.

Beneficiaries understand the ploy and do not object. In return for their high incomes and growing wealth, they are willing to be publicly attacked and denounced by the politicians. American federal administrations now commonly preach a form of populism while their policies enrich the wealthy. This pattern of political behavior is a fundamental reason why future financial crises cannot be avoided. American administrations are unwilling to seriously reform Wall Street — concentration of the financial industry, excessive speculation, over-leverage, all continue with government acquiescence. These factors are direct contributors to financial crises.

Examples of How Public Concerns are used to Benefit Insiders

A global example: The effort to ameliorate climate change

Many people have been informed of the potential dangers of changes that are occurring in the world's climate. International organizations, politicians, some scientists and the media have given climate change a high priority on the list of public problems. In consequence, regulatory and spending programs of various sorts have been devised to counter climate change. Many insiders are gaining from the efforts — including scientists doing research, entrepreneurs receiving government subsidies of various sorts, speculators dealing in permits for emissions; and politicians offering exceptions to regulatory requirements.

The need is made justification for the spending and programs whether or not there is any significant progress regarding the need. Not much progress is being made against climate change. In consequence, insiders press for more programmatic efforts and more funding.

Climate change thus becomes a perfect insiders' game. A real public concern is used to justify programs that benefit the establishment. Little or no progress is made on the problem. Lack of progress becomes a reason for more programs and spending. Always insiders benefit financially.

The Chinese know the game, but do not bother because CPC insiders can enrich themselves without pressing environmental protectionism. Theirs is a major manufacturing nation and emission restrictions threaten to raise costs and limit production.

This is not an argument that climate change is not a real problem requiring a public response — it may well be exactly that. But the insiders' approach does not resolve the problem; it merely benefits the establishment.

An American Example: The Affordable Care Act

The classic pattern of insiders is to identify a public need and propose programs to address it that can be exploited for the benefit of insiders. In this case it is a need in the United States for full coverage of the population by insurance for medical care. A large government program — the Affordable Care Act — has been enacted to rectify the situation. Some of the elements of the program are useful and significant. But misleading statements have also been made about the program to gain public support. Commitments have been made by the program's sponsors that are not intended to be kept. False promises have been made about the program's economic impact (which appears to be largely negative). The program has been enacted and adverse consequences are occurring, which accompany limited progress against the social need that was originally identified for correction.

Meanwhile a bureaucracy necessary to implement the program is being put in place; some insiders (especially insurance companies in this instance) expect to gain a great deal. So perhaps do medical care providers many of which have been exploiting existing federal medical programs (Medicare and Medicaid) for years. For example, in the middle of 2014 the *New York Times* reported that a single physical therapist had billed Medicare for over $4 million for one year's work.[8]

The result is higher taxes, job loss and reduction in economic growth. The government spends much more and borrows to pay.

The need initially identified was real; the government's performance in correcting it was very limited, most benefits go to insiders, and the cost of the small progress made to the middle class that pays taxes and purchases medical care is very high.[9]

An example from China: The failure of China to redirect its economy to a consumer-driven system

It is obvious to all including the Chinese that China needs to change its economic approach. For decades it has relied on two drivers of rapid economic growth. The first is technology transfer intensive manufacturing production which is out-sourced from the developed countries and the infrastructure of shipping (by road, rail, air and sea) which makes outsourcing possible. The second is rapid urbanization with its accompanying need for the construction of infrastructure — housing, roads, schools, shopping centers, railways, airports, etc. These two factors result in an investment-driven economy.

But China's manufacturing costs are rising and it cannot as easily expand outsourcing as it did in the past. Hundreds of millions of people have relocated from the villages to the cities and even China is now beginning to run low on people who can relocate to the cities.

Thus, both sources of economic growth — manufacturing for export and urbanization — in China are flagging. China needs to make a transition to a new driver of economic growth. The obvious candidate is

---

[8] Creswell, Julie and Gebeloff, Robert (2014), "One Therapist, $4 Million in Medicare Bills in One Year — Physical Therapy is a Big Recipient of National Medicare Dollars — and Physical Therapists in Brooklyn are among the Biggest Billers of All, Government Data Indicates". *New York Times* (April 28).

[9] References the CBO Study on the Impact of the ACA on Employment. Retrieved from http://www.aei.org/article/health/cbo-obamacare-is-a-tax-on-work-may-cut-full-time-workforce/?utm_source=today&utm_medium=paramount&utm_campaign=020514#. UvJsWqhV5TM.email.

personal consumption. This is the American model — an economy driven by the spending of consumers.

But China cannot get the transition done. Talk and programs do not lead to success. The programs enrich Chinese insiders, who are largely party members. The economic transition does not occur, while Chinese leaders promise that it will, and their well-wishers in the West insist that success will appear in the future.

Instead of the new economic model that stresses consumer spending, newly announced "reforms" ease emigration from the country to the city. The purpose of this is to give more impetus to the old economic driver which consists of urbanization and the construction of infrastructure. This is a retreat to the urbanization part of the old system. The manufacturing part of the old system which relies on outsourcing from abroad is not so readily revitalized, so that the Chinese rate of economic growth is slowing significantly.

Why cannot China make this transition which would so much benefit its people? Aside from technical obstructions, Chinese insiders benefit so greatly from the current system from which they are well-positioned to enrich themselves that the system is strongly resistant to change.

A form of approach to public problems that guarantees failure

The US began a war on poverty in America in the mid-1960s and has not waged it successfully. But hundreds of trillions of current dollars have been spent and thousands of bureaucrats employed, some insiders enriched, and many politicians advantaged. The UN and other international organizations have been fighting poverty and pursuing economic development in Africa for more than 50 years, and have not succeeded. But hundreds of billions of dollars have been spent and thousands of bureaucrats employed, some insiders enriched, many politicians advantaged.

This is how the insider-dominated system works. Insiders in the governments of developed countries and of international agencies identify a worthy goal and promise to achieve the goal if enough money is put into the effort. Programs are launched. In decades-long efforts insiders benefit from expenditures but the objective is never achieved.

Chapter **9**

Treadmill of Regulation

Economic crises are difficult to prevent in the west because politocrats prioritize tweeking regulations over fundamental reform. This can be described as a treadmill of regulation where publically touted reform initiatives are merely pretexts for enriching the privileged and furthering their political agendas. The point can be vivified by reviewing the financial and banking "reforms" undertaken in the wake of the 2007–2008 global financial crisis. To many commentators and political officials enhanced banking regulation seems the most significant route toward avoiding future crises. It is not.

Regulation of Banks as an Inadequate Response to Crises

Financial and bank crises are not merely a consequence of what happens in the financial sector of the world economy. They arise out of causes both economic and political in the world economy generally. Hence, financial crises cannot be controlled only by regulations applying to banks and other financial institutions.

Yet many countries are trying to prevent another financial crisis by relying almost exclusively on bank regulation. Regulators seem to be placing primary reliance on efforts to avoid failure in the chain of financial obligations that link banks to one another. Many popular commentators on the causes of the financial crisis of 2007–2008 have stressed the failure of major banks such as Lehman as a major cause in creating the crisis. The notion seems to be that if major banks can be strengthened so that they do not fail, then a crisis can be avoided. A chain is only as strong as its weakest link; the thinking seems to go, so the way to strengthen the chain is to strengthen its links.

However, bank failures in the 2007–2008 financial crisis were merely a proximate cause of the crisis, not one of its root causes.[1] The more important causes are remote from the banking industry and have not been successfully addressed; indeed, they cannot be successfully addressed by bank regulators who lack the jurisdiction and the authority to do so.

It is as though a great flood threatens to break through a dam. Water begins to seep through at many points. As the seepage grows into streams of water breaking through the dam, the entire structure begins to fail. The banking system is like the dam. The build-up of pressure on it arises from financial positions of governments, corporations, individuals and banks that cannot be sustained. Some banks begin to fail. But failure could come at many points, just as in the dam. If some points were stronger and resisted failure, other points would give way. The proximate cause of the failure of the dam is a set of specific leaks; the real, and remote, cause is the unrelenting pressure of flood waters against the dam. The proximate cause of the failure of the financial system is the collapse of a few banks; the real, and remote, cause is the build-up of unsustainable positions by speculators and governments. Under these pressures, if one bank does not fail, another will.

Hence, improved bank regulations alone cannot stave off another financial crisis, even though leaders pretend that bank reform is sufficient.

New Regulations on Banks will not Prevent More Crises

Banking regulations newly enacted after the financial crisis of 2007–2008 are having a significant impact on banks, though not a significant impact on the likelihood of another financial crisis. The new regulations complicate decision making in banks. New risk restraints make it difficult for banks to put seed capital into new aspects of their businesses. New insider trading regulations have caused some hedge fund operators to quietly close shop and leave the industry, hoping to escape the notice of prosecutors.

---

[1] Mian, Atif and Sufi, Amir (2014), *House of Debt*, Chicago: University of Chicago Press.

New conflict of interest regulations have impacted employees and potential employees of banks in many ways. All this is expensive, time-consuming, and irritating to bank executives and employees without having much impact on the risk of a new financial crisis.

The US reforms which were intended to avoid another crisis are those embodied in the Dodd–Frank Act of 2010 and the subsequent rules issued by various regulatory agencies pursuant to the Act. By and large the Act fails to meet its publicly proclaimed purpose. For many reasons it would fail to prevent, in backward glance, the 2007–2008 financial crisis, and it seems unlikely to prevent a crisis in the future.

In essence the Act does not sufficiently regulate the shadow financial system and instead continues to focus on the banks; it fails to restrain sufficiently government-sponsored enterprises; it fails to prevent financial institutions from shopping for regulators or from seeking to find gaps in regulation that can be are exploited to increase leverage; it provides a mechanism for rescuing financial institutions that are too big to fail, but does so with excessive bureaucracy so that a process that must be rapid is likely to be slow; and it promises to avoid future tax-payer bailouts of financial institutions, but the funds for this purpose do not seem to have been provided.[2]

Governments on the surface appear to be doing some right things. New regulations that require banks to have higher capital accounts and borrow less money (that is, employ less leverage) may reduce the likelihood of bank failures.[3]

Also, government regulators, especially the Federal Reserve, are much more active in regulating big banks. On the surface what attracts most attention is the increase in capital requirements which is being done largely by adding back into the calculation of liabilities many items that were allowed to be excluded in the years of deregulation.[4] But the

---

[2] See Acharya, Viral V. and others, eds. (2011), *Regulating Wall Street: The Dodd–Frank Act and the New Architecture of Global Finance*, New York: John Wiley and Sons.

[3] Team, Trefis (2014), "BofA forced to suspend 2014 Capital Plan due to Error in Ratio Calculations", *Forbes* (April 30). Retrieved from www.forbes.com/sites/greatspeculations/2014/04/30/bofa-forced-to-suspend-2014-capital-plan-due-to-error-in-ratio-calculations/.

[4] Armour, Stehanie and Tracy, Ryan (2014), "Big Banks to Get Higher Capital Requirement Increase in Leverage Ratio will require the Eight Largest Lenders to Add $68 Billion to

regulators are also putting their own professional employees inside the banks, which was not done before, to monitor transactions closely from inside the banks.

However, governments are claiming too much for regulation. In general, the claims are three:

1. That so much progress has been made in regulating financial markets that there will not be another financial crisis;
2. That proposals are being made to strengthen further the regulations and make crises even more unlikely;
3. That there is little or no likelihood of another financial crisis and what possibility there may be is declining because of regulators diligence.[5]

The flaws in these claims are substantial. Regulation of financial institutions does not negate government action that promotes financial asset price bubbles and which lead in turn to financial crises. The core of the matter is that the basic problems are not subject to resolution via financial regulation. They require basic reforms at a very high level of government and business.[6]

There was a significant preview of what is going to happen in the next financial crisis during the last one. On September 23, 2008, on Capitol Hill testifying before the Senate Finance Committee, Hank Paulson, Treasury Secretary and former CEO of Goldman Sachs said, "I was shocked to discover how ineffective financial regulation has been".

Level", *Wall Street Journal* (April 8). Retrieved from http://online.wsj.com/news/articles/ SB10001424052702303456104579489643124383708. "Still, some regulators expressed concern that the rule, which treats all assets equally when it comes to measuring risk, could provide an incentive for banks to load up on riskier assets or divest safer ones".

[5] Burne, Katy (2014), "Borrowing Cash to Buy Complex Assets is in Vogue Again Banks are Offering Leverage to Investors in CLOs ahead of Rules that Limit Holdings", *Wall Street Journal* (May 4). Retrieved from http://online.wsj.com/news/articles/SB100014240527023 03948104579537903377231522?mod=WSJ_hp_LEFTWhatsNewsCollection&mg=reno64-wsj&url=http%3A%2F%2Fonline.wsj.com%2Farticle%2FSB100014240527023039484810 4579537903377231522.html%3Fmod%3DWSJ_hp_LEFTWhatsNewsCollection.

[6] Lachman, Desmond (2014), "Ratings Agencies have Learned Little from their Errors", *AEI* (May 14). Retrieved from http://www.aei.org/article/economics/international-economy/ ratings-agencies-have-learned-little-from-their-errors/?utm_source=today&utm_medium= paramount&utm_campaign=051414#.U3PEXp3hGvE.email.

Paulson's comment brings to mind a scene in the movie "Casablanca". The French police chief stands in Rick's (Humphrey Bogart's) bar and says loudly, "I'm shocked! Shocked! To learn that there's gambling going on here!" As the police chief turns to leave, Rick's assistant appears and hands the police chief an envelope full of money and says something to the effect of, "Here is your winnings from your last visit". The complete hypocrisy of the police chief, who gambles at Rick's and yet pretends to be shocked to learn that gambling goes on there, amuses the audience.

Similarly, Paulson and his associates at Goldman and other Wall Street banks had been for years exploiting the ineffectiveness of financial regulation. Some of the methods the banks had used had just led to the financial crisis of 2007–2008, and now Paulson was pretending to have known nothing about all that. "I was shocked", he pretended, "to discover how ineffective financial regulation has been".

The media reported Paulson's comment without pointing out the hypocrisy, and Senators on the Committee also played along.

The details of financial regulation are now somewhat different than in 2008–2009, but the outcome is almost certain to be the same. Banks will find ways to circumvent many regulations, and the likelihood that malefactors will be punished for their speculative abuses remains miniscule. The circumventions plus the general inadequacy of banking regulation to the challenges of the marketplace will lead to ineffectiveness. Another financial crisis will occur.

Reform is Needed and Could do Much More than Regulation

Since the financial crisis of 2007–2008 many nations have enacted laws and regulations with the ostensible purpose of preventing a re-occurrence of the crisis. In the United States a voluminous law (the Dodd–Frank Act) imposed multiple new restrictions on banks advantaging some at the expense of others. The Dodd–Frank Act explicitly permits bailout — at government's discretion — via the law's resolution authority provision.[7]

---

[7]Pethokoukis, James (2014), "Is Dodd–Frank harming America's Startup Culture?" *AEI* (February 25). Retrieved from http://www.aei-ideas.org/2014/02/is-dodd-frank-harming-americas-startup-culture/?utm_source=today&utm_medium=paramount&utm_campaign=022614. The bailout would be financed by taxes on surviving banks and then

This means that "too big to fail" is now institutionalized giving large banks a competitive advantage that shifts the burden of distress on to the shoulders of smaller banks.[8]

In Europe, there have been somewhat similar restrictions placed on banks. Some of the new provisions are useful — especially increasing the capital requirements on banks. But many others are simply closing the barn door after the horse has escaped.

Significantly, most of the financial practices which led to the 2007–2008 crisis have been resumed by the banks. They were not prohibited by the new regulations. Instead, certain details of their conduct were modified.

In essence, the financial sector has been subject to different regulation; it has not been fundamentally reformed.

This is an important distinction. Regulation and fundamental reform are not identical, although many people presume that they are one in the same. Regulation and fundamental reform overlap to the extent that regulation can be used as a means of achieving reform. But for the most part, additional regulation is a substitute for fundamental reform. We regulate what we do not fundamentally reform. Fundamental reform means the behavior stops; regulation means we try to constrain the behavior. Fundamental reform is about changing structure and incentives; regulation is about rules as to what behavior is permitted. For the most part bank regulation — with its fines and penalties — is viewed by many executives and investors as merely a

---

potentially by taxpayers. Too big to fail is still here. Indeed, megabanks have responded to Dodd–Frank's TBTF incentives by getting bigger, the industry more concentrated. The six largest banks in the nation now have 67% of all the assets in the US, up 37% from five years ago. Second, by doubling down on TBTF, Dodd–Frank makes life harder for the rest of the banking industry. This is particularly the case for small banks.

[8]Pethokoukis, James (2014), "Is Dodd–Frank Harming America's Startup Culture?" *AEI* (February 25). Retrieved from http://www.aei-ideas.org/2014/02/is-dodd-frank-harming-americas-startup-culture/?utm_source=today&utm_medium=paramount&utm_campaign=022614. Since the second quarter of 2010 — immediately before the July passage of Dodd–Frank — to the third quarter of 2013, the United States lost 650, or 9.5%, of its small banks. Small banks' share of US banking assets and domestic deposits has decreased 18.6% and 9.8%, respectively, and the five largest US banks appear to have absorbed much of this market share. Mounting regulatory costs threaten to accelerate the shift towards big banks and away from small banks that have long been important members of the financial industry and the local communities they serve.

cost of doing business. In 2013, J. P. Morgan Chase Bank paid some $20 billion in fines, penalties and restitution for alleged violations of law and regulations. The result was that its stock price rose and its top executives remained in place. Apparently investors thought that even billions of dollars were merely a cost of doing business. The regulations had been in place; the behavior had continued. The regulators stepped in; the bank paid fines. The investors endorsed the executives. Not much was accomplished in the public interest by the regulation except some restitution. If the matter were part of a slide into a financial crisis, as it may turn out to be, then the regulations will be seen to be inconsequential.

Thus it is that regulation is often ineffective. Regulation generally affects the form rather than the substance of the causes of a financial crisis.

Fundamental reform is a substitute for regulation. It is a more extensive matter than regulation. For example, the separation in the 1930s of commercial and investment banking in the United States was a significant reform. It made it unnecessary to regulate in detail many of the practices which commercial banks engage in today because then — the commercial banks were not permitted to engage in those practices.

Similarly, trading on their own account as banks now do could be ended by reform rather than simply marginally restricted by regulation as the Volcker Rule seeks to do. Volcker had proposed a reform; what is being done is a regulation. The difference is critical.

The difficulty with regulation as a response to the financial crisis is that bank executives are ordinarily able to find ways to honor the details of regulations while failing to honor their spirit. Detailed regulations do not prevent many of the practices which banks engaged in leading to the financial crisis 2007–2008. In fact, almost all those practices are now resumed.

Professionals in the American Government recognize that another financial crisis is inevitable. It is recognized among top professional (if not political) officials of the American government that the Dodd–Frank Act will not prevent another financial crisis, and they are discussing both privately and publicly how the government should behave when it occurs. Officials note that the provisions of Part I and Part II of the Dodd–Frank Act will not prevent the need for another taxpayer bailout because the "living will" provisions that require big banks to have a plan for orderly liquidation in a crisis (so they can be safely placed into bankruptcy proceedings) are inadequate. Further there is no international bankruptcy law sufficient to sort out a big bank.

Also inadequate are the capital reserves which banks must hold under new regulations. This is because derivative obligations of banks are off their balance sheets and so the banks do not have capital reserves against them. Measured by international accounting standards only about 60% of bank assets are on the balance sheets of the banks. Taxpayers will have to provide liquidity in a crisis — private capital will not be available because it will not be able to calculate the value of collateral offered by banks for loans, just as happened in the financial crisis of 2007–2008.

Almost all the excesses of the financial sector prior to the last crisis are back and worse than before. For example, federal deposit insurance is again subsidizing proprietary trading by the banks. The concentration of assets in the big banks is greater than before. Excluding derivatives, the six or so biggest financial firms have about 65% of all US banking (and near-banking) assets; including derivatives the concentration of assets to about 80%.

There will definitely be another crisis, and when it comes it will be worse, officials admit. This is because the biggest financial firms are now larger, more concentrated, and more interconnected than before the last crisis.[9]

Failure to Make Fundamental Reforms

The financial reforms that are necessary to minimize the likelihood of a new financial crisis are:

- To reduce the size of the big banks, so that a failure in the chain of banks by one or two oversized banks will not cause a crisis in the whole system.
- To increase the capitalization of the big banks so that they are less likely to fail under pressure.

---

[9]See for example, various speeches of Thomas Hoenig, Vice Chairman, Federal Deposit Insurance Corporation. *The Economist* adopts the position that monopolies are alright and that governments should simply regulate their behavior. This is an open invitation to politocratic exploitation; and it doesn't work to protect competition and economic growth.

The Economist asks: "Should digital monopolies be broken up?" It answers, "Google is clearly dominant,… but whether it abuses that dominance is another matter…European politicians…should regulate companies' behavior, not their market power." (*Economist*, November 29, 2014, p. 11).

- To reduce the concentration of financial assets so that there is less exposure to the collapse of one or two institutions.
- To reduce the creation and trading of derivatives because the risks are high and imperfectly measured, so that some financial institutions are possibly endangered by their derivative portfolios.
- To reduce the syndication of loans because some of the loans are fragile when the economy turns down, putting institutions that hold many syndicated loans at risk of failure.
- To reduce speculation in financial markets because speculation is so large (possibly 90% of all trading is primarily speculative) and risky that it endangers the stability of the system.
- To reduce banks trading on their own accounts because the risk can endanger the solvency of the banks.
- To reduce the leverage (degree of borrowing) of banks and financial institutions because small turndowns in asset values can erase banks' capital and make the banks insolvent.
- To end the freedom of banks to buy other types of businesses and become in effect, conglomerates.
- To reduce the amount of borrowing by consumers because a downturn in the economy can make many people unable to service their debt, adding rapidly to the severity of the downturn.
- To reduce loans made without adequate collateral because a change in perception of the stability of these loans can cause a rapid collapse of their value leading to a general credit crisis.
- To reduce the volume of loans made to people without the income to properly service the loans because these loans are very risky and their perceived value can collapse suddenly, leading to a general credit crisis.
- To alter the business model of the credit ratings firms so that ratings are less susceptible to conflicts of interest of the credit rating firms.[10]
- To increase investment efficiency and spur growth.[11]

---

[10] Martin, Timothy (2014), "Ratings Firms Ride Bond Resurgence", *Wall Street Journal* (April 23). "The revival is due largely to the absence of any major changes to the industry since the financial crisis, including a business model that is blamed for contributing to the meltdown".

[11] Smith, Vernon L. (2014), "The Lingering, Hidden Costs of the Bank Bailout", *Wall Street Journal* (July 23). Retrieved from http://online.wsj.com/news/article_email/vernon-l-smith-the-lingering-hidden-costs-of-the-bank-bailout-1406160075-lMyQjAxMTA0MDI wNDEyNDQyWj.

Today, more than six years after the onset of the financial crisis, only a few items in the list of thirteen above have been even partly accomplished. In America there is less mortgage lending to people who cannot properly service the loans because of income limitations. But subprime loan lending is rapidly on the rise again,[12] and what were once mortgage practices have been appropriated by automobile retailers.[13] Expensive cars can now be purchased with no money down and loans cover not only the entire price of the vehicle but sales taxes, registration fees and maintenance contracts as well. The credit rating of the buyer affects only the interest rate she or he pays on the loan, not the availability of the loan itself.

Bank regulation associated with the Volker Rule is attempting to reduce banks trading on their own accounts, but congress has just underwritten trading losses on derivatives![14] Progress was made on several other items in the list in the immediate aftermath of the crisis, but it has now evaporated. Far from pursuing the reforms necessary to dramatically decrease the risk of another financial crisis, some central banks are doing the opposite.

For example, in mid-2014, the European Central Bank and the Bank of England expressed concern that the shrinking of the market for asset-back securities was imperiling economic recovery in Europe. Since abuses of asset-backed securities, in particular subprime mortgage backed

---

[12]Fannie, Mae and Freddie, Mac (2014), "Deconstruction Delays: A Flawed Reform of America's Housing-finance Market", *Economist* (March 22). Retrieved from http://www.economist.com/news/finance-and-economics/21599372-flawed-reform-americas-housing-finance-market-deconstruction-delays.

[13]Stansberry, Porter (2014), "A Big Concern ... Another Subprime Bubble, Already? ..."., *S&A Digest* (March 14). Americans owe $783 billion against their cars and trucks. Unbelievably, 34% of this debt is now owed by subprime credits.

[14]Moore, Heidi (2014), "Congressional Budget Welcomes Big Bank Bailouts Once More Despite White House Opposition", *The Guardian*, December 10. Retrieved from http://www.theguardian.com/business/2014/dec/10/congressional-budget-big-bank-bailouts. "In a small provision in the budget bill, Congress agreed to allow banks to house their trading of swaps and derivatives alongside customer deposits, which are insured by the federal government against losses. The budget move repeals a portion of the Dodd–Frank financial reform act and, some say, lays the groundwork for future bailouts of banks who make irresponsibly risky trades."

securities, was a prime cause of the 2007–2008 financial crisis, this position of European central banks may be considered remarkable.[15]

Non-financial reforms necessary to avoid new economic crises are primarily reductions in the size of governments, ending of dysfunctional regulation of private economic activities, increasing business competition, and dramatically reducing insider profiteering from governmental activities. The government is a primary source of economic disequilibria that pressures banks.

Capital Markets are Now Casinos and Do Investment and Credit Allocation Badly

John Maynard Keynes once commented that when the task of capital allocation in an economy is done by a casino, it is likely to be badly done. He was exactly right. The allocation of capital to productive uses is central to economic growth. To allocate capital effectively is the central social function of capital markets. The other social function of capital markets is to provide liquidity for investors — that is, to enable them to sell their investments for various reasons of their own. The primary capital market raises funds for new business ventures and for new business facilities. This can be done by loans or equity investments. The secondary capital market facilitates the sale of existing investments. It provides liquidity to owners of investments who wish to sell them; it does not provide investment capital ordinarily. It facilitates the operation of the primary capital market.

Bank regulation is now so extensive and complex that it interferes with the banks' function of loaning capital to business organizations. Instead, big banks find it more profitable to lend excess reserves to the Federal Reserve for interest payments and to speculate on their own account in the world's capital markets.

In all markets there is a useful role for a limited amount of speculative buying and selling. Some speculation helps markets function effectively.

But speculation in the world's capital markets today is massive and has long-since passed any useful level. As the world has grown richer in the

---

[15]Lawton, Christopher and Buell, Todd (2014), "Central Banks Say Regulations May Undermine Europe's Economic Recovery: ECB, BOE Concerned about Shrinking Market for Asset-Backed Securities", *Wall Street Journal* (April 12).

long period of peace that has followed World War II (since the Cold War never came to generalized fighting), there has been a huge build-up of savings. To a very large degree the employment of the build-up of capital has been in speculation, not investment. This is what hedge funds do; it is largely what private equity funds do. It is somewhat what mutual funds do. Capital today moves very quickly. Large companies see their average investor holding shares for less than one year. In general intermediaries (hedge funds, mutual funds, pension funds) interface with corporate management, not the owner of the capital (the potential investor). Modern capital markets operate like casinos in which players bet on short-term events. Markets function in the context of very low interest rates and asset price bubbles. It is a Wall Street adage that when the winds are strong even turkeys fly. The point is that with continuing speculative bubbles financed by central banks through low interest rates, turkeys will continue to fly until there is a crisis and winds of collapse cause the turkeys to fall.

Keynes would view modern capital markets as extreme examples of the casino he was describing in his comment made some 80 years ago.

The result is that today capital markets negatively impact the world economy in two substantial ways:

1. They do a poor job of allocating capital to productive uses — not enough gets to significant places, so that global economic growth is hindered; and
2. They generate economic instability via financial crises arising out of excessive speculation.

Since Summers and Krugman and many political leaders claim Keynes as authority for deficit spending to stimulate the economy, they should also embrace his condemnation of the adverse impact of Wall Street on investment and long-term economic growth.

How the Dynamics of Response to Crises Undermines the Opportunity for Reform

The financial crisis of 2007–2008 has not been followed by significant reform which addresses the underlying causes of the crisis. This is not by accident. It is a consequence of the political and economic dynamics of the response to a crisis.

Crises are not events; they are made up of events. Crises are processes in which events occur. Each crisis is a different process, though all have similar elements. The peculiar process of a crisis — its dynamics which include its economic events and the political response to it — determine what happens in the crisis to each of us and shapes our future.

For example, the prospect for the alleviation of a crisis and the prospect for the next crisis (its timing and severity) are inversely related. The sooner a current crisis is alleviated by emergency methods, the less attention is likely to be given to fundamental cures. The result is that the next crisis is likely to be more severe. What is needed is that a crisis be addressed with fundamental cures rather than emergency methods, so that further crises can be avoided.

Emergency efforts to alleviate a financial crisis — such as bank bailouts in the United States and the European Union — to the extent that they succeed actually undermine the potential for real reform. As the crisis fades, special interests reassert their political influence in a context in which politicians are relieved that the crisis is ending and business as usual is resuming. All involved want the atmosphere of crisis to end quickly. Yet significant reforms cannot be made except in a crisis situation and if the crisis is quickly ended, so is the momentum for reform. Hence, paradoxically, the more rapidly a financial crisis is alleviated, the more likely the next crisis becomes because reforms will have been avoided.

It is often observed that a crisis is a terrible thing to waste — that is, the opportunity for reform created by a crisis is something that should not be wasted if one wishes to avoid repetition of crises in the future. Unfortunately, throwing public money at a financial crisis — especially in the form of bailouts — shortens a crisis and alleviates its economic and political pressures, thereby squandering the opportunity for reform.

Reform does not happen automatically in the aftermath of a crisis. It is folly to expect democratic governments to do what they should do in the best long-term interests of the electorate. Instead, since reform can usually occur only in the midst of a crisis, it is the responsibility of democratic leadership to press reform as it acts to alleviate a crisis. The worst thing the government can do is give priority to immediate efforts to alleviate the crisis while pushing off reform to a later date. Fundamental reform then will not happen.

The story of the Dodd–Frank Act amply demonstrates this. The Dodd–Frank Act as proposed was supposed to embody significant reforms in the financial sector. It passed as a conglomeration of regulatory changes. Today, despite the Act virtually all the same actions which led to the financial crisis are now being repeated and the only question is when and with what severity the next financial crisis will occur.[16] The best that can be said for the Dodd–Frank Act is that it may have given the government better tools to confront the next financial crisis. If that is so, then paradoxically, the Act will have made the likelihood of real reform even more remote by more quickly alleviating the pain of the next crisis. What we have to look forward to is a continuing stream of financial crises the full ramifications of which we cannot see. Disaster of an economic or geo-political nature could accompany any crisis.

Going back to the conditions that led to the financial crisis

Perhaps today's economists and public policy makers are not as self-deluded. Perhaps today's economists and public policy-makers recognize that their favored policies are doing harm — to the world economy.

---

[16]Calomiris, Charles W. and Haber, Stephen H. (2014), *Fragile by Design: The Political Origins of Banking Crises and Scarce Credit*, Princeton, NJ: Princeton University Press.

   "It is challenging to assemble a winning coalition of like-minded people able to over-come the opposition of those that already control banking policy. Crises may mobilize constituencies for change, but powerful interests often succeed in using the crisis to strengthen their power. That was the result in 1913, when the Federal Reserve was founded to facilitate the operation of a fragmented banking system rather than to address the structural problems of unit banking. In the 1930s, instead of addressing the vulnerability of the banking system to agricultural income fluctuations and unit banking — the primary sources of bank failures in the preceding years — bank regulatory reforms further pro-tected small, rural banks by instituting federal deposit insurance and new regulatory limits on bank consolidation. The regulatory reforms of 1989–1991 wound down insolvent savings and loan associations and tinkered with regulatory capital requirements without actually constraining banks' and government-sponsored enterprises' abilities to undertake risk at public expense. In fact, banks made ample use of the new capital-requirements framework to build the hidden risks that revealed themselves in the 2007–2009 subprime crisis. As of this writing, the reforms introduced in the wake of that crisis have done little to end the subsidization of housing risk, to prevent banks from continuing to abuse the same system of capital regulation to hide risks in the future, or to prevent too-big-to-fail bailouts. Indeed, Title 2 of the Dodd–Frank bill enshrined and institutionalized those bailouts while pretending to get rid of them".

This would seem to be part of the motivation for the Federal Reserve System's current tapering of its policy of quantitative easing — the purchase of massive amounts of mortgages. The medicine of QE seems threatening to seriously harm the economy.

The asset price bubbles being blown in the economy by excessive credit ease are now threatening to severely damage the economy, and so must be restrained even though the stated purposes of the FED's easing (increased employment, lessened unemployment, renewed economic growth) have not been fully achieved.

The purpose of the FED in QEs is to re-inflate the housing market. The FED believes that banks are not making ordinary loans available to consumers or small business; so consumers and small business have to use home equity loans to finance consumption and business. If the FED inflates housing prices, then people can borrow and spend. This will get the economy growing. This is the FED's stated thinking and purpose.

The FED is trying to add to the debt burden of both households and SMEs (small and middle-sized firms). The FED is trying to recreate the conditions of excessive debt and insufficient personal and corporate savings which contributed greatly to the 2007–2008 financial crisis for the purpose of augmenting aggregate demand in the economy. This is precisely the opposite of what Krugman and Summers themselves insist needs to be done.[17]

The FED should instead be encouraging de levering (that is, lessening debt), encouraging savings, and thereby laying part of the foundation for a higher rate of real economic growth. Debt reduction would help avoid the creation of over-indebted governments, households and SMEs which is likely to contribute to the next financial crisis.

The FED is doing exactly the opposite of what it ought to be doing in the economy. Why? Is the government confused; ignorant; misled? More likely its actions benefit insiders and are so motivated.

In part by their own policies Congress, the President, regulatory agencies and the FED created the conditions that caused the last financial

---

[17]See their endorsement of Mian and Sufi, *House of Debt*. Retrieved from http://press. uchicago.edu/ucp/books/book/chicago/H/bo17241623.html.

crisis (bad lending in the subprime market and overleveraging by banks and consumers). They are now causing similar conditions to reappear for consumers and some large businesses — bad lending in the automobile market and excessive borrowing by consumers generally. The banks, on their side, are stronger today than immediately before the 2007–2008 financial crisis despite a resurgence of subprime lending.[18] But banks are again speculating strongly in financial markets. The return to practices very similar to those which contributed to the 2007–2008 financial crisis is intentional; it is sponsored by government leaders and agencies, and is justified in the same manner as before — as a necessary element of macroeconomic policy aimed at revitalizing the economy. The outcome will probably be the same — another financial crisis.

We are returning as a matter of policy to the conditions that led to the 2007–2008 financial crisis, hoping this time that tighter regulations on banks will be sufficient to avert another crisis. They will not.[19]

---

[18]Christies, Les (2014), "Subprime Mortgages Making a Comeback", *CNNMoney* (March 21). Retrieved from http://money.cnn.com/2014/03/21/real_estate/subprime-mortgages/.

[19]Daven, David (2014), "The Next Financial Crisis is Brewing Right Now, and Regulators are Missing It", *The Fiscal Times* (July 3). Retrieved from http://finance.yahoo.com/news/next-financial-crisis-brewing-now-093000636.html. "You may not see it on the front pages of your newspaper, but close examination will reveal an extreme unease from banking regulators about the current trajectory on Wall Street".

The Office of the Comptroller of the Currency (OCC), not typically seen as a strident regulator, is warning about risky lending as low interest rates drive a reach for higher yields. Both the OCC and the Federal Reserve have decried the slippage in underwriting standards on particular loan products. Fed Chair Janet Yellen cited "pockets of increased risk-taking" in a speech yesterday. And the Bank for International Settlements (BIS), a consortium of the world's central banks, cautioned this week about asset bubbles forming throughout the global economy.

The housing bubble fueled the last financial crisis, but these current risk pools largely sit in our capital markets. Regulators agree that newly issued corporate debt, a record amount of it below investment grade, has built up well beyond comfort levels. Investors bought as many so-called "leveraged loans" — junk bonds that offer a higher return because of the higher risk of default — in 2013 than they purchased from 1997 through 2012 combined. Debt-to-earnings ratios for these high-risk companies have risen to a post-recession high. Demand has been so elevated, in fact, that the spread between "high yield" corporate debt and risk-free securities like Treasury bonds fell to all-time lows, making it even crazier to purchase chancy debt for a small additional reward.

Weakness of Government Leadership in the Financial Area

Financial regulation alone cannot avoid oncoming economic crises. Significant reforms are needed. But deregulation without reform is also

---

Adding to the breakdown in underwriting standards, non-bank firms like hedge funds are performing a growing share of traditional bank activities, like providing corporate loans. As everyone seeks market share, lending quality loosens. These alternative lenders sit partially outside the regulatory perimeter, making it harder to ensure safety throughout the system. But they use the kinds of lending vehicles, like corporate bonds and derivatives, that oversight regimes that can track the police.

You can argue that protracted near-zero interest rates have driven a lack of stability in the markets. Federal Reserve officials will have a difficult challenge creeping out of the corner into which they have boxed themselves. But that argument overlooks a couple of key points. Raising rates and thus subjecting the economy to permanently depressed output due to concerns about financial stability not only could prove counter-productive, but it also neglects the other tools available to address the problem. In particular, as Yellen said in her speech, macro-prudential supervision and regulation, through direct oversight of the market and interventions to limit risk, can effectively promote stability.

This means that the primary regulators responsible for the capital markets — the Securities and Exchange Commission (SEC) and the Commodity Futures Trading Commission (CFTC) — carry increased importance, as the rolling ball of Wall Street risk has moved into their spheres.

While Dodd–Frank did not go far enough to deal with a changing market environment, it gave these regulators some increased tools to identify problems and move to stamp them out. Unfortunately, neither the SEC nor the CFTC have taken full advantage of these tools under their new leadership teams in President Obama's second term. If anything, they are rolling back the regulatory apparatus, increasing danger for the rest of us.

SEC: Slow in Enacting Changes.

SEC Chair Mary Jo White, a former federal prosecutor, came to the agency with a reputation for tough enforcement. But she had little regulatory experience, and predictably, that is where the SEC has lagged its counterparts. Watchdog group Public Citizen recently examined the official "Agency Rule List" to track the SEC's progress in writing regulations demanded by Dodd–Frank and found that well over half of the SEC's proposed rules have missed deadlines over the past year.

These delays include long-awaited action on asset-backed securities, exchange-traded funds, derivatives and market execution facilities, many of which comprise just the areas where risk has begun to accumulate. In addition, the SEC has for years avoided reforming the credit rating agencies, which gave their blessing to toxic securities that failed during the crisis. While there have been murmurs of impending action, they come far too late. "This is an unacceptable pace for rulemaking", said Lisa Gilbert, director of Public Citizen's Congress Watch.

very risky. It is worthwhile to recall that deregulation in America without reform set the stage for the 2007–2008 financial crisis.

Deregulation of financial services had the foreseeable consequence of industry consolidation. It was not deregulation to get more competition, but the opposite — to permit the creation of very large banks.

Alan Greenspan as Chairman of the Federal Reserve System of the United States championed deregulation of financial services firms. Greenspan has declared that he did not realize there was speculation that was driven by emotion ("animal spirits" as he termed them).[20] Greenspan seemed to think of the economy entirely in terms of macroeconomic models. He blames his failure to foresee the coming financial crisis on his failure to recognize that emotions (what he once referred to as "irrational exuberance") play a role in financial markets.

It is remarkable that a person with such lack of practical perception could be made Chairman of the American Central Bank. Greenspan famously said he had believed that the market would discipline financial institutions so that regulation could be relaxed. By his own admission he clearly did not know enough about the economy or financial markets to be in a position of such importance.

Similarly, Timothy Geithner, Chairman of the New York Federal Reserve Bank and then Secretary of the Treasury has admitted that he neither saw the 2007–2008 financial crisis coming nor anticipated its severity.[21]

What was Greenspan doing at the head of the FED? What was Geithner doing at the head of the Treasury? Why was each appointed? It is likely that each was appointed to serve insider interests that now dominate government — not to serve them directly but indirectly, via support for such actions as deregulation of financial service firms, in Greenspan's case, and to bail out the banks, in Geithner's case (he takes primary credit for the bank bailouts in his book *Stress Test*). From the perspective of the public, having people in office such as Greenspan, who are ignorant of the basic characteristics of the financial

---

[20] Greenspan, Alan (2013), "Why I didn't See the Crisis Coming", *Foreign Affairs* (November/ December). Cf. Shiller, Robert (2000), *Irrational Exuberance*, Princeton: Princeton University Press.

[21] Geithner, Timothy F. (2014), *Stress Test*, New York: Crown.

markets — for example, the major role that group emotions play in trading — who rely on theory — for example, that the markets can regulate themselves — rather than practical knowledge, should make people feel less not more secure about the future.

The same situation prevails today. The essence of FED policy is to keep interest rates low in order to support consumption spending by increasing the value of assets, in particular homes, so that people can borrow against them. This policy has at least three significant features:

(1) It increases leverage (that is, borrowing) in the economy when excess leverage was a key cause of the 2007–2008 financial crisis;
(2) It invites large banks and other financial market speculators to continue and even increase their speculative activities when these activities were another key cause of the 2007–2008 financial crisis; and
(3) It encourages private borrowing abroad toward unsustainable levels, another contributing cause of the 2007–2008 financial crisis. In the last few years (2011–2014) public debt of most developing (emerging markets) nations has been slowly declining. But the private debt — borrowed from abroad — has been skyrocketing to very large sums exceeding public debt. Private borrowing is sustaining economic growth — though at lower rates than in the past. The borrowing is contingent on continuing low rates of interest which are the result of the actions of the American FED. Hence, a shift in American monetary policy toward higher interest rates will imperil economic growth in much of the developing world.

Effectiveness of leadership is an element of the response to financial crises. Poor leadership yields bad results. And will again unless the west weans itself from the treadmill of insider regulation.

Chapter **10**

Macroeconomic Miasma

Macroeconomic miasma has crippled the response to financial crises and undermined economic growth. Politicians, scholars and citizens want to believe that employment, aggregate economic activity, growth, wages, prices, and interest rates not only can be explained by a few elementary variables, but can be precisely controlled by monetary and fiscal policy. They want to believe that the macroeconomy is transparently deterministic, is easily determined for the common good and therefore that the machinations of insiders should they occur are of little consequence. This desire has created a toxic atmosphere (miasma) enabling politarchs to degrade and warp the economy for their private purposes, while claiming to wisely mix monetary and fiscal policies in response to the popular will. Macroeconomic miasma provides an excuse for excessive state and private leveraging is a principal cause of the west's failure to prevent economic crises and decay.

Such thinking seems epidemic in the United States and Europe. Respected economists engage in it; the media picks it up from them and broadcasts it; politicians echo the economists and the media. When pressed, reputable economists admit their errors, but continue to repeat them publicly. The result is occult policy-making that is damaging the world economy. The exaggerated efficacy of macroeconomic is doing great damage.

The deficiencies of contemporary macroeconomics are legion, including: flawed data, econometric indeterminism,[1] fuzzy theorizing, incomplete theories, omitted variables, conceptual opportunism and political expediency. These deficiencies are discussed below.

The Significance of Macroeconomics Today

Macroeconomics is a body of theory and data which applies to national economies as whole entities. Macro means large — macroeconomics deals with the large elements of economies — not with specific industries or companies or geographic areas. Macroeconomics provides data about total production (GDP), employment, redundancies, aggregate price levels (CPI and WPI). It provides a body of theory to analyze macroeconomic data for the purpose of making forecasts and policy.

Macroeconomics is relatively recent construct. In its current form it was popularized by John Maynard Keynes in two books written in the mid-1930s addressing the problems posed by the Great Depression. Keynes was dealing with a very specific situation — which he fully recognized and clearly stated. The problem was considerable unemployment caused by underproduction. The western economies then had massive under-utilized resources of all kinds — labor, natural resources, manufacturing facilities, and transportation systems. In this context, Keynes advocated government deficit spending to put people and resources to work. This was the original proposal for macroeconomic policy.

But at the time Keynes wrote, data on national economies were scant. So policy was made in the dark — so to speak.

This problem was resolved by harnessing the national income accounts which were then being designed, but intended for very different purposes. As always, politicians were impatient, so that although proper data were not at hand, available information was pressed into service — the national income accounts. This pattern of impatience we will later see continues to this date and takes many forms. The major work was done at Harvard, and the United States led in the preparation of the accounts. This is where today's GDP figures originated. In part because the data were best

---

[1] Some policy analysts claim that policy should be determined solely by the best econometric results, with further expert knowledge. See Meltzer, Alan H. (2014), "Too Much Hype Chasing Too Little Wisdom," *Claremont Review of Books*, pp. 48–51.

fitted to other purposes, they provide considerable error when used for purposes of political economy. To accompany GDP figures surveys were designed that collected employment and unemployment data.

Most people assume that macroeconomic data are built up from more specific data, what are called micro (small) economic data. That is, people presume that macroeconomic data can be completely disaggregated. Since we have national unemployment data, it is presumed that we can give the level of employment in Atlanta, for example. We cannot. The national data are often based on limited survey data that have a certain reliability at the national level, but not when disaggregated.[2]

---

[2] Johnson, Rodney (2014), "The Sun Always Shines at the BLS", *Economy & Markets* (June 18). However, the BLS does not survey every business. That would be a massive undertaking. Instead, it samples a small portion of existing companies.

The choice of what companies to include is not completely random. Given that over 27% of private employees work for companies with more than 1,000 employees, the BLS skews its sampling to the larger firms. Never mind that those companies represent only 0.2% of all US firms.

This makes sense if you are trying to simply count workers, because it allows you to capture the most workers using the fewest survey results. But that is not the point of the monthly jobs report. Instead, the BLS is trying to capture the change in employment. While layoffs often happen at big companies, the process of adding workers is skewed to the smallest firms. And that is where the fight starts.

While the BLS surveys more than 60% of the companies with over 1,000 employees, the agency surveys fewer than 3% of the companies with less than 50 employees, even though more than 30% of employees work for such firms.

The issue, of course, is that there are so many small companies. Trying to survey the bulk of them would be inefficient.

So the BLS makes up for the small sample size by adjusting the weight it gives each small company in its survey, but even this does not completely do the trick. With such a small sample size of small firms, the BLS understands that it can miss important hiring data.

To compensate, the BLS uses historical data to guesstimate how many new employees were hired by small firms, how many new companies were formed, and how many went out of business.

This total adjustment is called the Birth/Death Adjustment, and is added to the Non-Farm Payroll numbers each month.

Keep in mind that these are not jobs the BLS has counted, or knows exist, they are simply guessed at.

If the BLS estimates that more people went to work at small firms or started new companies than were let go, then the Birth/Death Adjustment is positive. But theoretically, the number could go either way.

A Peculiar Conceit

The result of this is a peculiar conceit held by many prominent macroeconomists. The conceit is the notion that one can fully understand

---

While there have been a few months here and there where the BLS showed a negative Birth/Death Adjustment, in the overwhelming number of months the adjustment is positive.

The latest employment report is no different, and is a great example of all the BLS's guesswork. 217,000 net new jobs were created during the month, which sounds great! But a quick look at the Birth/Death Adjustment raises questions. In this guessed at category, 207,000 jobs were created. This means the BLS actually counted only 10,000 net new jobs, but estimated that uncounted new positions at small businesses added the rest.

However, the guesstimates do not simply carry into the future. Every January the BLS matches up its work with that of the Census Bureau, taking a hard count of how many people are working in the population.

If the BLS has undercounted gains in employment during the previous year, it will add more workers to the January Non-Seasonally Adjusted numbers. If it overcounted employees during the previous year, it will subtract workers from the January Non-Seasonally Adjusted numbers.

In January of 2014, the BLS adjusted down the numbers by 307,000.

This negative adjustment, which is used to unwind overoptimistic employment numbers from the previous year, is the norm. From 2010 through 2013, the adjustments were −427,000, −339,000, −367,000 and −314,000.

Notice a trend? Every single year the BLS had to unwind some of its over-the-top optimism about the number of jobs created.

Of course, these after-the-fact corrections that happen each January do not make it into the headline number, even though the original, erroneous estimates are plugged right into the headline each month.

It would stand to reason that if your entire job was estimating employment in the US each month, you would want to be as accurate as possible, with very little correction necessary each January.

As such, it would make sense that the error (because there will always be some, of course) would fall on both sides of the zero line, requiring a positive correction in some years and a negative correction in others.

But not at the BLS. In that organization it appears that the goal is to do what you want with estimates, as long as the effect is positive. If it has to be backed out in a future month, no worries! Most people do not pay attention to those changes down the road. I guess in that sense, the BLS could change its name to the Font of Useless Numbers, or FUN.

At the end of the day, the problem is that people use employment numbers to gauge the health of the nation, both in a snapshot and as a measure of trend.

If we are constantly fed rosy numbers that must be adjusted lower each year, then we are consistently being misled about the health of the nation.

For the millions of unemployed and underemployed, I am sure none of this comes as a surprise.

the national economy without understanding its elements. The notion is similar to a physician insisting that she can fully understand the human body while knowing nothing about its components. In fact, physicians understand that this is not true, and instead attribute knowledge only to the specialists. Economists do the opposite and the politicians are fine with that.

The result is that we have a group of economic and political leaders who prescribe policy for economies about which they understand very little, and possibly care less.

Limitations of Macroeconomics — Analysis and Policy Prescriptions

For these reasons, macroeconomics is inadequate to the tasks of modern economic policy. The problems of developed economies cannot be resolved by policy prescriptions based on macroeconomics primarily or only. Modern economies cannot even be adequately understood in terms of macroeconomic theory, regardless of the availability of adequate and accurate data. This is because the tools and concepts of macroeconomics are too few, too blunt, too over-used, too short term, and too ineffective to stimulate growth and general prosperity. Macro data are inadequate and inaccurate. Economic conditions cannot be interpreted accurately without considerable supplement by microeconomic data. But most economists pay little or no attention to micro data — such as corporate reports and industry-specific and occupation-specific data — presuming that the creators of macro data have consulted micro-information in preparing the aggregate (macro) data.

The economist who developed modern macroeconomic models was once asked at Harvard about the confirmed inaccuracy of much of the data his statistical models were employing to generate forecasts for the government and for big businesses. He acknowledged that the data were flawed. He was then asked if he and his firm would assist in trying to get the data improved. His answer was, "We are not concerned about the quality of the data. We simply use it".

It is this mind-set that is so damaging to efforts to resolve today's economic problems. Much economic data are unreliable but many prominent economists ignore the consequences of this. The data seem precise — the unemployment rate is 6.3%, for example; or the GDP of the

United States is $16.23 trillion — suggest a precision which they lack; it is a false precision. But to many people who are unacquainted with the limitations of the data, the apparently precise numbers imply correctness. The false suggestion of accuracy is very similar to the use of detailed narratives by journalists to suggest accuracy in the broader aspects of a story. In both, detail is used to imply accuracy which is entirely missing from the main elements of the story.

Probably the worst offender in the realm of economic statistics at this point is the indices which purportedly measure the rate of inflation of consumer goods. Those indices have for the past few years registered very little inflation. Yet most shoppers perceive a very different reality. There are three major reasons why the rate of price inflation is probably much higher than reported by the official statistics:

1. Pricing for measurement purposes of products which are not important in the shopping of consumers;
2. Inflation hidden by a proliferation of products and services in which minor variations in the product or service are represented as significant improvements and are made the occasion for a significant price increase;
3. Explicit underestimation by adjustment of the data as measured.

The professionals and technicians who prepare price indices are aware of each of these sources of downward bias and periodically attempt to adjust information collection for them. At the present time they appear to have fallen seriously behind in providing an accurate index of price changes. What is most significant is that government policy makers and pundits ordinarily accept the official statistics as gospel and cite them as reasons for proposed macroeconomic policies.

There are three key elements of modern economic policy-making:

• Understanding the functioning of the economy;
• Statistical analysis including its methodology; and
• Formulating policies to deal with economic challenges.

It is common for economists today to do the second two without ever bothering with the first. The best known economists, the most Nobel prize-heavy, are experts in statistics (econometric modeling) and policy discussion. They seem remarkably ignorant of the actual functioning of modern economies. Worse, they seem not to care about reality. In the face of unrelenting errors in forecasting, they continue to forecast in the same way; in the face of the continual failure of policy measures, they prescribe more of the same. They are a modern form of the medieval scholastics — placing primary emphasis on dialectical reasoning to extend knowledge and policy by inference. Their work is known for rigorous analysis and heated debate. They have added to their medieval predecessors' approach today's rigorous statistical analysis. But today's economists are as uninterested in empirical reality as were their predecessors. Challenged on this point the most prominent modern economists will always point to macroeconomic statistics as evidence of empirical evidence — which it is, to a very limited degree.

Because economists in the current macroeconomic tradition are so limited in knowledge of economies, though not of neoclassical economic theory, they are not equipped to anticipate, avoid and deal effectively with financial crises. They are methodologists not realists. But they love the public attention and political prominence afforded by pontificating about economic policy and they are not embarrassed by decades of failure to improve the performance of modern economies.

Economists and politicians have now led us into a round of debates about whether what today's circumstances require is economic stimulation (that is, more government spending) or austerity (that is, efforts to reduce government deficit spending). Stimulation means further government spending financed by borrowing as a means of generating economic activity. Austerity means cutting back government spending as a way of reducing debt and interest payments. The debates are heated and sound to the public to be very sophisticated technically. In reality, they are devoid of significance for addressing today's economic problems. When politicians and macroeconomists argue over the best way to resolve modern economic issues, they are not really discussing how to solve problems, but instead are contesting whose supporters will bear the costs of their respective approaches.

The problem for the public is that the most prominent economists and politicians have allowed the miasma macroeconomic theorizing to cripple their thinking. To address the challenges of financial crises and economic stagnation effectively we must junk an entire generation of politicians and their economic advisors whose thought and mental categories are the outdated concepts of macroeconomics. To successfully approach the risk of continuing financial crises we must turn to a more robust version of modern economics, one which is more complex and inclusive than macroeconomics.

This is not to say that macroeconomics is not useful for certain purposes — in particular the analysis of the direction of fiscal and monetary policies — and that it is not especially valuable in certain economic conditions — in particular, deep depression. But modern economic problems are a consequence only partially of poor fiscal and monetary policies and the problems can be addressed only very imperfectly by macroeconomic policies. Macro has its uses, but the macro strategies currently favored are counterproductive.

The reason why macroeconomics cannot resolve our problem of on-coming financial crises is simply stated. The problem is the result of both bad macroeconomic policies (fiscal and monetary) and of the increasing stagnation of the world's economies (which is the concern of microeconomics). Hence, macroeconomists ignore a major factor involved in causing the problem — the stagnation of major economies. Rather than investigate stagnation with proper tools, including microeconomics and inclusive economics, macroeconomists simply treat stagnation as resulting from macro concerns — fiscal and monetary policies. Their proposed solutions, therefore, are seriously incomplete. As we have seen in Chapter 3, this does not concern the politicians who profit from the onset of the world's economic problems and from the attempts made to resolve them.

Bleeding the Patient

In the 18th century, in which we can find useful analogs for today's world, a group of people presented themselves as physicians.[3] They responded to

---

[3] For example, when England's King George IV was Regent for his father in the second decade of the 19th century, he experienced a spell of serious illness. During the course of his sickness his doctors drew from his body several pints of blood. When he recovered — which we know today was not because of their bleeding him, but in spite of it — the physicians announced to the world that their repeated bleedings had cured him. Had he died, they would surely have said that they had not bled him enough. Similarly, today if our economy were to show signs of life, our policy-makers will attribute it to their high spending/

many illnesses with the same treatment — drawing blood from the patient. Blood was drawn in a variety of ways — among them incisions and the application of leeches to the patients' bodies. Patients had two problems to recover from — their original disease and the bleeding done by their physicians. Some patients recovered from the bleeding; many died. But the physicians failed to get the lesson from the deaths of many patients. The weaker a patient became — the more the physician bled him or her. The physician believed that by removing blood from the systems of his patients, he was helping to cure them. Instead, he was weakening his patients so much that many died of his treatment. The physician remained blissfully unaware that his treatment was killing his patients, or if he was aware, he denied it vigorously because the treatment was all he knew how to do and he earned his living by it.

Many of today's economic pundits are similar to 18th century bleeders — they prescribe more and more of the same medicine despite clear evidence that the patient is dying from it. They bleed the economy by excessive government spending, the build-up of debt, by taxes, waste, and regulation.

The metaphor of the bleeder is ghastly, but so is what the politicians and their macroeconomist aides are doing.

A recent example can be taken from discussion in Australia. When there is not a program of regulatory reform and incentive creation (or regulatory permission) to revive private investment and spending, then cutting a government budget deficit will threaten economic growth because government spending is driving the economy.

The result is this kind of thinking: "Australia's government needs to be careful not to cut spending too deeply in next month's budget for fiscal 2014–2015, as the economy still faces major challenges, a member of the central bank's policy board told *The Wall Street Journal*. Some economists have warned that the budget is shaping up as a risk to growth, providing a further headwind to an economy already facing a slowdown in mining investment". Thus, spending is necessary because the nation's leaders have no other mechanism to address a problem of inadequate demand. Deficits

---

high debt policies. If our economy continues to stagnate or begins to decline, they will surely insist that there was not enough borrowing and spending.

are killing the economy over the long-term, but deficit spending is the only treatment they have. So more of it.

Macroeconomics is the economics of the 1930s. It has been kept alive because it can be made to seem to offer various rationales for very large government spending. The purpose of the spending is to enrich insiders, but it is sold to the public as a means of providing entitlements, assuring full employment, avoiding recession and stimulating growth. It does not matter if Spain has perpetual double digit unemployment, or that the real source of sustainable growth is technological progress. The only thing that counts for policy-makers is that people are inclined to believe that government spending provides a free lunch. Since macroeconomic tools do not provide a route to economic growth other than the temporary fillip from speculative leveraging, over time the economy stagnates and experiences both financial crises and recessions. As this circumstance continues, more resources flow to insiders and the public generally experiences increasingly difficult times.

Chapter 11

Dogmatism

Macroeconomic theory as Keynes stressed in the introduction to his *General Theory* rests on the assumption that the economy is in equilibrium everywhere except the labor market.[1] The supply and demand for all goods and services, the composition of employment, prices, wages and the interest rate are all competitively efficient at every non-full employment level of aggregate activity (on various production feasibility frontiers),[2] but "sticky wages" prevent adjustment to competitive full employment.[3] Keynes famously claimed that this deficiency can be resolved with sufficient government deficit spending.

Macroeconomic theory thus rests on the premise that because markets are competitively efficient and Keynesian policy-makers know how to harness the "multiplier", full employment, general equilibrium and the prevention of crises can be achieved without adverse side effects merely by calibrating the right dosages of deficit spending. This for many is an

---

[1] Keynes, John Maynard (1936), *The General Theory of Employment, Interest and Money*, London: Palgrave Macmillan.

[2] Samuelson, Paul (1947), *Foundations of Economic Analysis*, Cambridge: Harvard University Press.

[3] Mankiw, Gregory and Reis, Ricardo (2002), "Sticky Information versus Sticky Prices: A Proposal to Replace the New Keynesian Phillips Curve", *Quarterly Journal of Economics*, Vol. 117, No. 4, pp. 1295–1328.

"infallibilist" macroeconomic position;[4] a "true" belief that cannot be doubted despite compelling counterfactual evidence. Other beliefs may be justified and more consistent with the evidence, but if they do not rise to the level of true belief in the eyes of the true believer, they are mistaken. Philosophers call this dogmatism an infallibilist fallacy. It provides yet another reason why preventing crises is so difficult. Too many economists who believe that markets are efficient and policy-makers adept cannot accept that they might be seriously mistaken even when their predictions are repeatedly falsified.[5]

Contemporary macroeconomic dogmatism does not necessitate a commitment to any particular version of Keynesianism, or fixed theory other than the belief that deficit spending and stimulatory monetary policy suffice to assure microeconomically efficient, crisis free full employment and vigorous economic growth. Once it is accepted that "prudent" stimulatory policies are indispensable then it is off to the races with ever bigger government programs, debt accumulation, credit expansion, leveraging and indulgent financial regulation, paving the way for secular stagnation and crises.

All that matters for politicians who reflexively assert that their policy and regulatory strategies are failsafe is that they can receive enough support from reputable experts to gull the public into passively accepting their claims that the invisible hand in the private sector and the state's visible hand together dependably assure technically efficient outcomes.[6] This allows partisans of most persuasions to contend that economics and politics is about satisfying their desires because they believe that there are no significant inefficiency costs imposed by deficit spending, government programs and loose monetary policy.

---

[4] Kuhn, Thomas (1996), *The Structure of Scientific Revolutions*, Chicago: University of Chicago Press. Karl Popper (1934), *The Logic of Scientific Discovery*, London: Routledge.
[5] Rosefielde, Steven and Pfouts, Ralph W. (2014), *Inclusive Economic Theory*, Singapore: World Scientific Publishers.
[6] Technical efficiency is a professional term for all points along Samuelson's production possibilities frontier. Supply at any of these points other the full equilibrium is efficient given counterfactual prices that could, but do not prevail. Most macro theorists conflate technical with full economic efficiency.

Macroeconomic dogmatism is pliable. "Right" beliefs can mutate to suit prevailing agendas.[7] In the 1960s Keynes's emphasis on over-saving and under-investment was replaced by an under-consumptionist hypothesis that allowed the American government to stimulate aggregate economic activity by substituting broad income tax cuts for investment subsidies.[8] During the first eight years of the 21st century, new-Keynesian macro-theorists claimed that thanks to "divine coincidence" it was possible to perpetually sustain full employment with 2% annual rate of inflation by judiciously controlling the money supply and the entire term structure of interest rates.[9]

The 2008 financial crisis shattered the illusion, but not the infalliblist faith in pliable macroeconomics. Today theorists are busily trying to construct a narrative where creating a credible lender of last resort forestalls crises no matter how great the stimulus,[10] and deleveraging necessitates continuous monetary expansion to counteract deflation.[11] The new key words are "supersized bank run" (stemming from the actions of non-bank banks), "deflation", "liquidity traps", and "balance-sheet recession".[12] The core claims are the insistence that supersized bank runs cannot occur if there is a credible lender of last recourse; the assertion that declining prices and wages are catastrophic (anti-austerity), and that household debt deflation driven by deleveraging is a powerful drag on aggregate effective demand. Hence, continuously expanding government stimulus and monetary ease to avert deflation and bolster flagging consumer demand is essential, a position now embraced by Janet Yellen. In an epoch of secular stagnation, it is suggested that the magnitude of government

---

[7] Rosefielde, Steven and Razin, Assaf (2012), "The 2008–2009 Global Crisis", in Steven Rosefielde, Masaaki Kuboniwa and Satoshi Mizobata, eds., *Prevention and Crisis Management: Lessons for Asia from the 2008 Crisis*, Singapore: World Scientific.

[8] Heller, Walter (1966), *New Dimensions of Political Economy*, Cambridge MA: Harvard University Press.

[9] Blanchard, Oliver and Galí, Jordi (2007), "Real Wage Rigidities and the New Keynesian Model", *Journal of Money, Credit, and Banking*, Vol. 39, No. 1, pp. 35–65.

[10] Diamond, Douglas and Dybvig, Phillip (1983), "Bank Runs, Deposit Insurance, and Liquidity", *Journal of Political Economy*, Vol. 91, No. 3, pp. 401–419.

[11] Razin, Assaf (2014), Lecture, Chulalongkorn University, Bangkok, June 24.

[12] The concept was introduced as "debt deflation" by Iriving Fisher in 1933.

and private debt can be safely increased without risking inflation, crises or microeconomic distortions.

The story line fits some of the facts and provides a fruitful framework for discussing policy. Macroeconomics is useful in this regard as long as the narrative does not cross the threshold into dogmatism. However, the emerging new hypothesis cannot withstand close scrutiny for two reasons. First, we do not know with certainty that "credible" lenders of last resort will really stave off traditional or shadow bank panics. Second, we do not know enough about deleveraging (as distinct from wage compression) to claim that tapering at the present juncture is either beneficial or counterproductive, while on the other side of the ledger we do know with confidence that contemporary stimulus tactics disequilibrate the microeconomy.

Some economists are open minded in this regard — even some who favor continued stimulus — but for most the attitude too easily hardens into dogma.

Chapter **12**

Pipe Dreams

Economic dogmas are strongly shaped by beguiling political pipe dreams compounding the difficulty of dispassionately averting the dangers of secular stagnation and crises. Insiders are adept at preying on people's idealism for their own purposes and imperiling national welfare.

The pipe dreams crafted by today's insiders are a toxic mixture of self-interest, wishful thinking, partisanship and utopianism. They take various eclectic, ideological and theocratic forms. Nazism and Soviet communist ideologies are gone, but softer pipe dreams remain.[1]

Daniel Bell presciently declared the age of ideology dead in 1960,[2] arguing that the appeal of grand 19th and 20th humanist schemes had been exhausted and would be replaced for purposes of political control by soft ideologies and eclectic ideals like "entitlements".[3] His prediction has come true for America, the European Union and a host of other developed western societies where insiders have found that they can pursue their self-interests best under the banner of slogans like "big brother" government, prosperity, growth, egalitarianism, equal opportunity, entitlements for the

---

[1] Krugman and Yellen perceive themselves as defenders of the "public good".

[2] Bell, Daniel (1960), *The End of Ideology: On the Exhaustion of Political Ideas in the Fifties*, Cambridge, MA: Harvard University Press. Cf. Jacoby, Russell (2000), *The End of Utopia: Politics and Culture in an Age of Apathy*, New York: Basic Books. Aron, Raymond (2001), *Opium of the Intellectuals*, Brunswick, New Jersey: Transaction Publishers. Fukuyama, Francis (2006), *The End of History and the Last Man Standing*, New York: Free Press.

[3] Bell, Daniel (1976), *The Cultural Contradictions of Capitalism*, New York: Basic Books.

deserving, affirmative action, women's and homosexual rights, multicultur-
alism, indulgent life styles, environmentalism, liberalization, globalization,
world government and perpetual national and international harmony.

Today's political pipe dreams lack the sophisticated artifice of Marxist–
Leninism and its beguiling claim of ineluctability, but exploit similar
emotional vulnerabilities. Most people identify themselves with socially
approved causes and insiders have learned how to accommodate them for
their private purposes. Their versions of the gospel arouse intense passions
and loyalties that make it extremely difficult to do the right thing.
Counseling fiscal rectitude and sound money for example is frequently
treated as apostasy. Austerity which imperils the interests of insiders and
speculators is dismissed by them as a benighted attacked on full employment and prosperity. Media hype compounds the problem.

Today's soft ideologies are best described as "ideocratic", a term
coined by Martin Malia forming a middle ground between 19th and 20th
centuries style ideologies and eclecticisms. He calls anti-Enlightenment
economic systems "ideocracies". The term is constructed from the roots
"ideo" (idea or ideal), and kratia (rule) and means any economic system
governed by an ideal such as perfect state planning or a moral imperative
like egalitarianism rather than free individual utility optimizing. Ideocratic
insiders champion plans over markets, the welfare of the "deserving" over
equal opportunity for all, and globalization on their terms. Because of
these preferences, they reject the freedom of the individual to make her or
his own economic and political choices. There is always room for blend-
ing planning and markets, the requirements of groups and the individual,
and competing international agendas but ideocrats carry things too far.

The "ideo" — that is, the key idea — can be as simple as full employment or as complex as democratic socialism or harmonious world government. The broad latitude allows ideocratic rulers to claim that markets are
inferior to whatever ideo they champion. Markets are said to do some
good, but cause much harm. Hence, they must be subordinated to wor-
thier purposes on a wide variety of ethical and pseudo-scientific grounds.
If enough people find these claims persuasive, or merely acquiesce, rulers
become "legitimately" empowered (by elections, public opinion polls or
passive acceptance) to pursue agendas on a sustained basis either as an act

of faith,[4] or as a subterfuge concealing their private self-seeking. Feudal potentates before the French Revolution were legitimated by the principle of divinely sanctioned social hierarchy (hierarchy of estates). Communists, following Marx's blueprint sought to establish their legitimacy by criminalizing private property, markets and entrepreneurship. Fascists did so by making nationalism and/or racial supremacy their guiding star, while European and American social democrats embrace the causes of global egalitarianism, minority empowerment, affirmative action, collective harmony and world government.

Malia and Max Weber insisted that feudal, communist, fascist and social democratic rulers seldom act in accordance with their professed ideals. They adhere more to the form than the substance of ideocratic dreams. For Malia and Weber neither rulers' dogmatic and unscrupulous behavior, nor the people's gullibility are baffling.[5] Hardnosed rulers and insiders are driven by their desire for wealth, privilege, power and the plaudits that come with pretending to be virtuous (honorable). Electorates are easily enthralled by grandiose visions.[6] Moreover, true believers are not

---

[4] Weber, Max (1978), *Economy and Society*, Berkeley, CA: University of California Press. Authorities legitimatize themselves by persuading critical segments of society to accept the righteousness of their ideas and ideals through charisma (Hitler), appeals to tradition (nobility), and rational-legal processes. Dahl, Robert (1971), *Polyarchy: Participation and Opposition*, New Haven: Yale University Press. Lipset, Seymore (1983), *Political Man: The Social Bases of Politics*, London: Heinemann. Schmitt, Carl (2004), *Legality and Legitimacy*, Durham, NC: Duke University Press. Legitimacy is the term used by political scientists to describe popular acceptance of governmental authority, including law. The concept can be extended to regimes where people acknowledge and acquiesce to authority without approval or consent.

[5] Everyone knows that utopia by definition is an impossible dream, and that no indisputably true or best morality exists, yet people are prone to believe that their notions of virtue, truth and justice are the only right ones.

[6] Ajemian, Robert (1987), "Where is the Real George Bush?" *Time* (January 26). Retrieved from http://content.time.com/time/magazine/article/0,9171,963342,00.html#ixzz2sjoQkyOw. George Bush acknowledged the power of political visions, but felt uncomfortable bothering with them. Ajemian, who interviewed Bush wrote: "This has led to the charge that he lacks vision. It rankles him. Recently he asked a friend to help him identify some cutting issues for next year's campaign. Instead, the friend suggested that Bush go alone to Camp David for a few days to figure out where he wanted to take the country. 'Oh', said Bush in clear exasperation, 'the vision thing'. The friend's advice did not impress him".

deterred by stark discrepancies between dreams and realities,[7] including both unfilled promises and failures. Ideocrats have relatively little difficulty convincing most contemporaries that secular stagnation, economic crises, national decay and international discord are merely temporary setbacks; that tomorrow will be a brighter day, and everyone must keep the faith and try harder. Pipe dreams in this way shape the dogmas that govern policies making secular stagnation and crises strongly path dependent.

Daniel Kahneman would have us believe that reasoned "slow thinking" soon corrects intuitive "fast thinking" idealism, but the durable appeal of ideocracy counter-suggests that he is mistaken.[8] Debunking destructive forms of idealism is a frustrating and ceaseless challenge.[9]

[7] Hoffer, Eric (2002), *The True Believer: Thoughts on the Nature of Mass Movements*, New York: Harper Perennial Modern Classics.
[8] Kahneman, Daniel (2011), *Thinking, Fast and Slow*, New York: Macmillan.
[9] Bartlett, Tom (2014), "Social-Psychology Researchers are very Liberal. Is that a Problem?" *Chronicle of Higher Education* (July 29). Bartlett provides evidence that social psychologists are overwhelming "liberal" and slant their analysis accordingly.

Chapter **13**

Doublethink

To know and not to know, to be conscious of complete truthfulness while telling carefully constructed lies, to hold simultaneously two opinions which cancelled out, knowing them to be contradictory and believing in both of them, to use logic against logic, to repudiate morality while laying claim to it, to believe that democracy was impossible and that the Party was the guardian of democracy, to forget, whatever it was necessary to forget, then to draw it back into memory again at the moment when it was needed, and then promptly to forget it again, and above all, to apply the same process to the process itself — that was the ultimate subtlety; consciously to induce unconsciousness, and then, once again, to become unconscious of the act of hypnosis you had just performed. Even to understand the word 'doublethink' involved the use of doublethink (George Orwell (1949), *Nineteen Eighty-Four*, London: Martin Secker & Warburg Ltd., London, Part 1, Chapter 3, p. 32).

Ingsoc's (English socialism) credo: *War is Peace, Freedom is Slavery, and Ignorance is strength.*

Doublethinking (now sometimes called "motivated blindness")[1] makes pipe dream policy-making nearly impervious to rational critique

---

[1] Bazerman, Max (2014), "Seeing What Leaders Miss", *Harvard Gazette* (August 8). Retrieved from http://links.mkt3495.com/servlet/MailView?ms=MTA1OTExMDYS1&r= MjA5MjgwODM5NTES1&j=MzIzMzc4MDM3S0&mt=1&rt=0. "Social scientists have long identified our tendency to overlook bad news when it suits us as 'motivated

and empirical disconfirmation, providing yet another barrier to overcoming secular stagnation and averting crises. People infected with doublethink often fall victim to pipe dreams even if they distain them. Worse still savvy professionals who appreciate the irony of the situation, nonetheless succumb to a subtler form of doublethinking by insisting that acting on false premises does not matter because everything will turn out for the best.

The claim that providence assures the best of all possible worlds is well entrenched in western culture. Gottfried Leibniz expounded the thesis in his 1710 work *Essais de Théodicée sur la bonté de Dieu, la liberté de l'homme et l'origine du mal* (Essays on the Goodness of God, the Freedom of Man and the Origin of Evil). Voltaire (François-Marie Arouet) satirized Leibniz's assertion in *Candide, ou l'Optimisme* (1759) to great acclaim, but with no lasting effect. Doublethink pipe dreams persist and have morphed into an instrument of insider state control.

George Orwell coined the term doublethinking in his dystopian novel *Nineteen Eighty-Four* to describe how people are conditioned to gull themselves into believing two contradictory things and acting as if mutual exclusivity were irrelevant in accordance with their indoctrination.[2] Doublethinking encompasses mendacity and hypocrisy, but emphasizes the process by which people avoid coming to grips with approved lies. People are brainwashed to know that something is false and yet reflexively believe that it is true, or to know that something is true and reject it as false. Failure to doublethink under "Ingsoc's" (English socialism) rule is a "thoughtcrime" (contemporary political incorrectness).

The doublethink driving today's global economic turmoil is the failure to acknowledge that an addiction to deficit spending, off-the-books expenditures (social security and various insurance schemes), monetary debasement, financial leveraging, pro-insider regulation, hidden inflation, insider transfers, a war on the productive middle class and reckless foreign

blindness', a term that refers to a systemic failure to notice unethical behavior in others when it is not in our interest to do so. The condition affects virtually everyone. Even leaders who have gained tremendous success through focus and application in one arena sometimes lack the self-awareness to routinely question whether information on which they are basing decisions is reliable".

[2] Orwell, George (1949), *Nineteen Eighty-Four*. London: Martin Secker & Warburg Ltd.

adventures is incompatible with competitive efficiency, Pareto neutrality and democratic sovereignty. Economists and politicians laud competition, self-reliance and consumer sovereignty (both over private and public goods), they attribute the west's success to democratic free enterprise, and the Soviet Union's extinction to its reliance on planning, regulation and administration; state dependency and systems directors' sovereignty, but doublethinking economists and politicians nonetheless claim that democratic free enterprise cannot function beneficially without the wise state's visible hand. They know that insiders do not wisely manage the economy and international relations, but this does not change their belief that the state manages wisely. They contend that interest rates are competitively determined, even though they know that the FED sets them.[3] They know that they cannot efficiently micro tax-transfer, but insist that they do the job right. They know that overregulation is lethal, but contend that the west cannot survive without it. They know that the private sector creates worthwhile jobs, but Hillary Clinton denies it.[4] They know that a war against the productive middle class is counterproductive, but cannot desist. They know that prices and wages should decline when demand abates (Walrasian price adjustment mechanism), but insist that deflation is an anathema. They know that over-taxation is economically and socially hazardous, but continue to overtax. They praise equal opportunity, but are addicted to affirmative action. They know that sooner or later the piper must be paid; that debts must be settled and that pandering to speculators is playing with fire, but assert that both are essential. They know that America has squandered trillions of dollars in futile wars against poverty, drugs and terrorism drugs for decades, but the spigot remains open. They know that America spent trillions on the Iraq War and

---

[3] Rosefielde, Steven (forthcoming), "Secular Crisis: The Mundell–Fleming Trilemma and EU De-Legitimation", in Bruno Dallago and John McGowan, eds., *Crises in Europe in the Transatlantic Context: Economic and Political Appraisals*, London: Routledge.

[4] "Don't let anybody tell you that, ah, you know, it's corporations and businesses that create jobs. You know that old theory, trickle-down economics. That has been tried, that has failed. It has failed rather spectacularly." Clyde Wayne Crews Jr., "Hillary Clinton: Businesses Don't Create Jobs," *Forbes*, October 26, 2014. Retrieved from http://www.forbes.com/sites/waynecrews/2014/10/26/hillary-clinton-businesses-dont-create-jobs-just-speaking-fees/.

related adventures abroad with even worse results, but the public passively acquiesces to throwing more good money after bad. They know that they cannot prove that their programs and transfers improve social welfare relative to the competitive benchmark, but aver that more is always better. They know that full employment, income equality and growth as reported convey a misleadingly positive impression of national welfare, but do not care. They know that high unemployment, extreme inequality and secular stagnation are the poisoned fruit of their policies, but deny it. They should know that current policies are making the west vulnerable to Russian and Chinese aggression, but refuse to accept the inference. They know that globalization is a code word for pax Americana, but refuse to blush. They know that they are willfully ignorant, but the euphoria makes it seem to them that whatever happens will be for the best. They are the sons and daughters of Leibniz and consummate doublethinkers.

This is no small matter. Leaders cannot muster the resolve to act constructively, if they are committed to the proposition that what is good for insiders is the right thing to do.

Part III

Framework for Sustainable Prosperity

Chapter **14**

The Importance of Inclusive Economic Theory

The antidote for doublethinking is inclusive economic theory,[1] that is, a unified utility-seeking framework that takes explicit account of idealist rational possibilities (both perfect markets and perfect planning), bounded rationality, non-rational selection, unscrupulousness, culture, ideocracy, reckless foreign adventures, miss governance, insider control, collective risk aversion and normative ambiguity to fully illuminate the possibilities of economic management. Economic activity broadly defined is any labor, productive or exchange operation that individuals, groups or collectives feel provides value added. If they are rational and moral in a comprehensive idealist sense, then value added should be beneficial, external diseconomies aside. If people non-rationally select, are psychologically disturbed, are unscrupulous, coerced or subjected to miss government and insider control, then gains may be illusory or negative in varying degrees.

The "utility" generated by individual, group and collective economic activities thus are difficult to calibrate not only for the usual ordinal and cardinal reasons, but for a complex set of additional psychological, sociological and ethical factors. This means that the merit of any economic

---

[1] Rosefielde, Steven and Pfouts, Ralph W. (2014), *Inclusive Economic Theory*, Singapore: World Scientific Publishers.

system, public policies and transactions cannot be adequately deduced with standard macro and microeconomic indicators on assumptions which presume systems are workably competitive, and governments democratically neutral or socially progressive. Standard indicators tell us something, but are only a starting point. They must be supplemented with information on anti-competitiveness, government insider self-seeking, collusive insider state-private "partnerships", and then evaluated from multiple individual, social and ethical perspectives to construct superior public policy.

This is the key message of "doublethink-free" inclusive economic theory. Politicians and economists (blind men) cannot adequately grasp the big picture by touching selected parts of the elephant,[2] and they cannot formulate right policies by assuming that only the elephant's ears matter. The elephant's complete anatomy must be comprehended. Right appraisals take account of the whole. All other approaches are one sided.

Inclusive economic theory makes no sweeping prejudgments. Instead it subdivides economic activity into three baskets: idealist, realist and neo-realist each operating according to its own laws and each requiring special forms of investigation. Idealist markets (and perfectly planned economies) that broadly satisfy the rationality and ethical conduct axioms underpinning neoclassical economic theory can be judged in terms of their competitiveness (Pareto efficiency). This includes perfect and some forms of imperfect market power. Realist markets governed by conventional ethics, bounded rationality and satisficing (as distinct from profit maximizing) must be assessed case by case to ascertain just how far and in what ways they depart from idealist neoclassical expectations.[3]

Neo-realist activities which relegate rational and ethical utility and profit-seeking searches to other goals cover the rest of the territory from

---

[2] Reference here is to the Jain, Buddhist, Sufi and Hindu parable of the blind men and the elephant. A group of blind men touch an elephant to learn what it is like. Each one feels a different part but only one part, such as the side or the tusk. They then compare notes and learn that they are in complete disagreement.

[3] In Herbert Simon's realist world consumers and producers want to rationally utilize and profit maximize, but find themselves in a non-satiation attractor space compatible with multiple heuristic satisficing solutions without a uniquely deterministic solution. They want to rationally optimize, but cannot do so.

cultural protection to dementia, the unscrupulous behavior of individuals and insiders and reckless foreign adventures. Much of the value added/subtracted is concealed in the neo-realist realm. People and governments are reluctant to disclose their misdeeds. The facts need to be unearthed, compiled and analyzed. It cannot be presumed that economic activity is efficient and just, or that insiders are well motivated. Quite the contrary, it is wisest to assume that economic activity is flawed and damage mitigation is policy-makers' only viable alternative.

The performance characteristics of economies governed primarily by ethically principled, competitive transactors (market or planned) adheres to the Paretian script. The actions of satisficers, cultural conformists, disturbed individuals and unscrupulous power seekers by contrast cannot be inferred from first principles and must be ascertained case by case.

This duality could mean that the merit of any system in the final analysis boils down to the extent of rational decision making, and that reform is mostly about expanding the scope of rational choice. However, this is misleading because governments do not have the capacity to perfectly plan (regulate). Technocrats do not know the economy's production functions and micro inter-enterprise dependencies. They do not have real time information on consumer tastes. They do not have the technical capability of accurately simulating perfect competition and cannot be adequately incentivized to do the right thing even if computopia were feasible.[4] Moreover, planners and regulators do not just underperform. They distort, impair, inhibit and overburden private transactors. Planning and regulation thus are intrinsically lose–lose, not win–win propositions, except for some basic services (including minimalist countercyclical macroeconomic stimulus). The notion that not-for-profit, anti-competitive state institutions can provide better outcomes than democratic free enterprise is absurd; a claim supported by the Soviet and North Korean test cases.

This inference applies in spades in the neo-realist domain where the personal motives of politicians, insiders and collaborators override those

---

[4] Neuberger, Egon (1966), "Libermanism, Computopia, and Visible Hand: The Question of Informational Efficiency", *American Economic Review* (March), Vol. 56, Nos. 1/2, pp. 131–144. Cf. Dixon, Peter B. and Jorgenson, Dale W. (2013), *Handbook of Computable General Equilibrium Modeling SET*, Vols. 1A and 1B, Amsterdam: Elsevier.

of the consumers, nations and the international community. Insider power-grabbing distorts, impairs, inhibits and overburdens as it did before, but now it is turbocharged by self-seeking. This compounds the magnitude of the productive losses and concentrates the burden on the productive middle class. Productive efficiency and growth potential are degraded causing secular stagnation, while insiders and speculators flourish.

The inclusive economic theoretic framework showcases the danger. This makes it more powerful than the neoclassical idealist and realist (bounded rationality) paradigms that conceal the risks of insider government by pretending that public officials are competent, vigilant and well-intended. Adam Smith understood the danger, but his insight has been obscured by modern counterclaims. Once, the lesson is rediscovered, it is easily seen that the right path forward is confining government to its proper role, increasing competitiveness, prudently applying fiscal and monetary stimulus, reining speculation and attending to a myriad of neo-realist issues.

The contours of sound democratic economic systems design and policy essential for financial stability, full employment, efficient production and distribution, and optimal GDP growth are well known. They are that governments should

- foster unfettered market competition,
- restrict leverage,
- repress financial speculation,
- shun public programs that can be achieved more cost effectively in the private sector,
- eschew all regulations where public costs exceed well-defined benefits,
- deficit spend and inflate the price level only to the point where the social benefit of increased production equals the associated costs,
- avoid reckless foreign adventures and provide an adequate national defense.

This is the only tried and true path to enhancing the public good.

Chapter **15**

Breaking Vicious Cycles

Avoiding crises, combating secular stagnation and deterring international conflict require that much be done because we are far along in decay. Inclusive economic theory demonstrates that we can go much further, and are likely to, but even at this point we are beyond the place of a quick and easy turn-around. This is because we are in a vicious cycle in which emergency measures and inaction justified or not follow one upon another and prevent us from making longer term improvements. For example, we cannot lessen public or consumer debt because we cannot accept a period of transition in which total spending is lessened as debt is retired. Hence, emergency spending measures (so called stimulus) crowd out longer-term debt reduction. Debt keeps rising and the emergencies become more serious. The emergency action is piling on debt and bloating the money supply. The inaction is failing to exercise self-restraint.

This is the dynamic we have described in this book. It is a downward spiral imperiling the world economy. It is worsened by the fact that emergency measures and inaction create their own constituency — those who benefit from them — both insiders in government and business who benefit in large amounts and people at the margin of society who benefit only a little but become dependent on the emergency measures. This group is growing rapidly in our Europe and America — measured as the long-term unemployed and those who do not look for work. The point is further confirmed by laments that America's more than half-trillion dollar projected budgetary deficit for 2014 is "irresponsibly" too small![1]

In this situation, with a string of emergency measures making long-term improvements impossible, and with the steady growth of a constituency for emergency measures, proposals to make long-term improvements are seen as radical. Proposals to cut government spending even a little, and to reduce, not increase the debt, are loudly denounced as irresponsible.

This is the most severe crisis — not its symptoms such as financial crises or recession — the unwillingness of governments to economically and politically do what they need to do (including international relations and defense) in the best long-term interests of the public good.

The most important reforms needing to be made with respect to the world economy are the following:

Be Objective about the Direction of the World Economy

Virtually every year international organizations, national governments and private business organizations predict a substantial improvement in the world economy; virtually every year those predictions are not met. But inaccurate predictions of this sort serve establishment purposes. People are led to believe that reforms are not necessary because the economy is getting better. As each year closes and it becomes clear that the positive predictions made at the beginning of the year are wrong, insiders propose emergency responses to right the economy. Hence, the emergency programs so profitable politically and financially to insiders are said to be working.

This is another powerful dynamic by which the purposes of the politocracy are attained. Year after year emergency programs occur and the situation deteriorates; yet nothing of a fundamental and long-term nature is done to resolve the underlying problems.

The beginning of a significant effort to improve the prospects of the world economy must begin, therefore, with an objective assessment of its

---

[1] Cooper, Ryan (2014), "Obama's greatest failure: The rapidly falling deficit: The falling deficit is a pointless exercise that has come at the cost of keeping millions out of work", *The Week* (July 3). Retrieved from http://theweek.com/article/index/264151/obamas-greatest-failure-the-rapidly-falling-deficit.

direction. This becomes more difficult each year because of increasingly inaccurate or misleading statistics. Therefore, two things are needed:

1. More comprehensive assessments of the world economy which official macroeconomic data are supplemented with observations and data at the industrial, company and regional geographic level. This requires the construction of formal models which can incorporate a variety of types of information. Until such models exist and are validated, we must rely more heavily on assessments based on informed judgment.

2. More up-to-date statistical definitions and collection methods for macroeconomic data. In particular, gross output estimates need to be refined to include only real value added, not rework, red tape, mistakes, fraud, etc. which now provide a significant part of the economic activity of developed nations. It makes no sense that when a clerk makes a mistake in filing a travel expense form, for example, so that a group of people must spend considerable time straightening the matter out, all the unnecessary effort is counted as productive labor in national income statistics. When there was much less of this, it did not matter much. Now there seems to be a great deal of non-value added in our economic statistics and we need to know how much to isolate productive increases in economic activity.

Objectivity regarding the economy will permit us to identify and address the basic causes of current and coming crises.

Strengthen the Productive Middle Class

A major source of initiative, work effort and spending each of which strengthens the world economy is the activity of the productive middle class. A key reason for the emerging stagnation of the world economy is the squeeze placed by the insiders of democracies on the productive middle class, now under assault as a new working class. The squeeze tightens daily, with distinct consequences which will be unfortunate. Strengthening the productive middle class requires stronger incentives for work and savings, the twin pillars of middle class status. This requires lower taxes generally and real returns on savings. Taxes now are generally being increased and savings receive minimal returns. Governments should support middle class savings, not engender increasing debt.

Assist the Poor

In the western democracies insiders continually promise to end poverty. Substantial sums are devoted to this objective, some of which reach the poor. It is unlikely that insiders can be driven from their positions of power if nothing is done for the poor.

The best assistance for the poor is economic opportunity. To provide this many things are necessary. First and foremost is a vibrant economy creating jobs offering good pay and benefits. Achieving this requires that government pay attention to the composition of modern economies, not simply to aggregate figures of total spending (gross domestic product (GDP), for example). Manufacturing and software programing, for example, provide high-paying jobs because jobs in those industries are supported by substantial capital investments. This is not true of lower level service and retail jobs, which are the sorts of jobs being created in disproportionately large numbers by the developed economies today.

Physical safety is necessary for people in low income areas to develop careers. Educational opportunity is required. A public culture is needed that supports working, rather than glamorizing drugs, sex and violence. In the developed countries the *de facto* residential segregation of the poor into jobless neighborhoods needs to be ended.

Public programs that support living standards and healthcare are needed, but today's mélange of fraud, graft, incompetence, inefficiency and ineffectiveness need to be abolished so that benefits reach the poor.

Shun Privilege, Affirmative Action and Entitlement

Efficient and productive societies require that citizens be self-reliant and have equal opportunity. Western societies today are proceeding on the opposite premise. They are cultivating privileges for insiders and their partners including big social advocates, while using profiling techniques to provide unwarranted entitlements and disability subsidies at the expense of the productive middle class. The strategy is wrongheaded because it necessarily degrades aggregate productivity and is socially unjust in the name of social justice.

End the Conventions by Which Markets are Controlled and Political Favors Purchased

Because insiders in today's large economies are sophisticated, there is little direct violation of law when the public interest is flouted. Open conspiracies remain illegal but are not necessary because implicit understandings among large firms obviate any need for them. Bribery is unnecessary because implicit understandings between politicians and lobbyists obviate any need for explicit *quid pro quos*. Courts in America and Europe seem oblivious to this development.

Laws against the manipulation of prices and quantities in markets and against the improper influence of political processes need to be expanded to cover understandings as well as direct instances of conspiracy and bribery.

Establish Competitive Markets

Law in the developed countries is now a tangle of protections for special interests and exemptions in their behalf. Most industries are concentrated in the hands of one or a few firms. It is argued that competition is protected because consumers have choice among substitutes and so there are multiple producers. Cable television is not a monopoly because one can purchase a satellite system instead. Microsoft does not have a monopoly because one can buy a cell phone instead of a computer. By this logic, a single airline would not be a monopoly because a consumer can drive instead of fly.

What is important is a return to competition among multiple producers in each industry in large national economies and in the global economy. This includes professional sports as well as communications and similar industry long protected from perfect competition.

Attaining competition will require a modification of inheritance taxes to permit family-owned firms to survive generational transfers; will require broad-purpose enforcement of anti-trust laws; and will require independence of capital sources from equity positions in companies to which they loan money (this is crucial until banking is far less concentrated an industry than it now is).

End Financial Industry Concentration

The concentration of the financial industry into a few very large firms is a major factor increasing the likelihood of further financial crises. This is true despite increased regulation of the banks. Avoiding future crises requires breaking up the large banks and careful regulatory oversight of the industry.

It is necessary, therefore, to apply anti-trust laws to reduce the size of the big banks by breaking the largest banks into competing businesses, so that a failure in the chain of banks by one or two oversized banks will not cause a crisis in the whole system.

Also, it is important to continue regulatory efforts to increase the capitalization of banks so that they are less likely to fail under pressure.

Smaller banks are less likely to engage in speculative activities in financial markets on behalf of themselves and their clients. When some banks fail due to speculation, they are less likely to be important enough to bring the system down in a crisis. Speculation, derivatization (that is creating and trading derivatives) and syndication are all less likely in a perfectly competitive banking industry and are less likely to cause a crisis when a bank or a few banks fails due to these activities.

Regulators have developed a variety of means to reduce speculation by financial firms. Among the means are high tax rates on short-term gains, limitations on borrowing (leverage) for speculative purposes and limitations on selling short. These should be employed aggressively until the proportion of speculation in total financial markets trading is reduced substantially below what it is now.

Return to Sound Money

Inflation in the world economy and in the economy of the United States (US) and Europe is much higher than is being acknowledged and reported officially. The build-up of bank reserves sponsored by central banks as an economic policy threatens very rapid inflation in the future and is already causing rapid inflation in some asset classes. Also, as nations pile up debt burdens the temptation to repay them with depreciated currency will become irresistible. Already discussion of such moves is being heard privately.

When lenders become more concerned about the value of their holdings of debt, a financial crisis will occur. This can only be averted by a return to sound money (very low rates of inflation) and by control of the volume of government debt, even though Janet Yellen has now promised easy money forever.[2]

Sound money combined with a pay-down of government debt by the US would, after an adjustment period, largely allow us to avoid the current high risk of further financial crises and subsequent recessions.

Decrease the Size of Government by Half

Reduction in the growing debt load of many nations is central to the minimization of the risk of future financial crises. The most direct method of achieving this is a major downsizing of the size of government. The reduction in public spending which is achieved by downsizing government can be used to eliminate budget deficits and reduce outstanding debt.

Whenever a proposal for decreasing the government's size by half is made insiders burst out with expressions of horror. A collapse of the nation's economy is predicted. The loss of valuable public services is predicted. One thinks of the old proverb — a stuck pig squeals.

Yet, when properly evaluated — when the propaganda, promises and false statistics of the politarchy are rejected and fully removed from our minds — then there is nothing substantial lost in the downsizing. What disappears is useless bureaucracy, fraud and insider enrichment — all of which now exist on an enormous scale. Government can be downsized with no loss to the public good. Already very important missions to which

---

[2] "Yellen says Fed easy money needed even after recovery: report", *Reuters*, July 14, 2014. Retrieved from http://finance.yahoo.com/news/yellen-says-fed-easy-money-needed-even-recovery-133651741--business.html.

government has pretended to devote itself, including national security, economic opportunity, elimination of poverty, and environmental improvement are not being accomplished, but instead are being exploited for insider enrichment. There is therefore nothing to be lost by cutting the government down to reasonable size.

Avoid Reckless Foreign Adventures and Maintain an Adequate Military Deterrence

The west is abetting the repolarization of world into two hostile camps; one democratic and the other authoritarian and militaristic. It is aggressively threatening Russia's national security interests by seeking to incorporate Ukraine into the European Union (EU) and eventually the North Atlantic Treaty Organization (NATO), while simultaneously degrading its deterrent capabilities and pretending that the Kremlin can be contained with economic sanctions and sweet reason. Its policies toward China and the Middle East are of the same mindset. Dampening global turmoil necessitates the opposite approach. The west must restrain itself from encroaching on the east's spheres of Influence, and deter them from expanding their domains.

Chapter **16**

Lesser Evil

There is very little room for fundamental disagreement about the state of the global economy and potential dangers such as rampant inflation, financial crises and global repolarization. We accept the Economic Policy Institute (EPI)/Summers–Krugman characterization of the core problems confronting America (US) and the European Union (EU): The prospect of a blighted future of substandard economic growth, stagnation or worse, exacerbated by abnormally high unemployment and underemployment, widening income and wealth disparities between corporate executives and workers (including the middle class), and deteriorating conditions for Black and Hispanic retirees. Likewise, we accept obvious trends toward cold war repolarization and increased armed insurrection in the Middle East, Africa and parts of Asia.

Therefore, the case for eradicating insider big government, state and private leveraging and foreign adventurism can only be challenged on three fronts. Critics can dispute our "facts". They can accept them, but counter argue that current practice is the lesser evil, or dismiss today's global economic turmoil as teething problems.

Disputable Assertions

The contestable assertions are of two different sorts. Critics can challenge our claims about (1) the wastefulness, incompetence, abusiveness and counter-productiveness of government programs and foreign initiatives, and

(2) policy-makers' motives and intentions. Regarding the wastefulness, incompetence, abusiveness and counter-productiveness, officials routinely assert that they are honest, responsible and competent. They insist that they do the job, and do it right. They acknowledge some errors (mostly due to factors beyond their control), waste, fraud and abuse, but contend that the problem is not large, and is under control. When political parties spar over budget cutting, all sides insist that there is little fat to cut. They contend that every executive order, mandate, regulation and program is essential, and point out that 65% of all federal budgetary expenditures are "mandatory" (entitlements).[1] Congress insists all government revenue and borrowed funds must be spent. Readers can judge for themselves whether government provides services efficiently,[2] or whether programs are worth the expense.[3] Anyone with experience in Washington DC or Brussels knows that they are neither.

The appraisal of intentions is similar. Politicians across the globe including the EU, China and Japan insist that they are competent, virtuous

---

[1] Boccia, Romina; Fraser, Alison Acosta and Goff, Emily (2013), "Federal Spending by the Numbers: Government Spending Trends in Graphics, Tables, and Key Points", *Heritage Foundation* (August). Retrieved from http://www.heritage.org/research/reports/2013/08/federal-spending-by-the-numbers-2013.

[2] Paul Light estimates that the Federal government could save one trillion dollars over 10 years by reducing management levels from 18 to no more than 6. Light, Paul (2011), "Opinion", *Wall Street Journal* (July 7). Specially, he recommends freezing all hiring at the senior and middle levels of government (possible savings: $250 billion); eliminate $300 billion delinquent federal income taxes owed by federal and congressional employees, contractors and stimulus recipients, streamline, focus on productivity, eliminate automatic time-on-the-job pay increase, cut contract employees by 500,0000.

[3] A Congressional oversight committee recently discovered that New York has overcharged Washington $15 billion for mental healthcare since 1990. Gershman, Jacob (2012), "State Accused of $15 Billion Fraud Scheme", *Wall Street Journal* (September 21). A congressional oversight committee on Thursday accused New York of overbilling Medicaid by billions of dollars by inflating reimbursement payments to its state-run institutions for the mentally disabled. In a scathing report, the Republican-led House Oversight and Government of New York charged a per-diem rate of $5,118 for residents of the institutions, a network of 11 centers that now house about 1,300 people with severe developmental disabilities. Over the course of a year, Medicaid spends $1.9 million for every resident or $2.5 billion in total — with half coming from the federal government. But the cost of running the institutions is only a quarter of that amount. "This is intentional fraud", said Arizona Rep. Paul Gosar, a Republican committee member.

and committed to deregulating, cutting the productive middle class's tax and compliance burdens, reducing deficit spending, repaying national debts, curbing credit creation to avoid rampant inflation, and promoting global harmony. Perhaps, but it is difficult to believe their promises because they never admit the limits of their competency. Only 19% of Americans today trust their politicians,[4] and respect for their competence is not much higher. The American people seem to understand that the government is not working for their good, and that insiders are placing their interests ahead of the public's, claims by politicians to the contrary notwithstanding.

The American government's behavior exemplifies the global trend. It has not reduced tax and compliance burdens on the productive middle class,[5] run budgetary surpluses (see Table 16.1), or maintained a neutral monetary stance for more than a decade despite its advocacy of these policies for others ("Washington Consensus"), although now and then words are uttered in support of all these objectives. The same can be said for the EU, China and Japan. It cannot be proved that Washington and other contemporary governments do not intend to reverse course at some point, but no major government has set forth a credible timetable for fulfilling their promises.[6] This silence is deafening and justifies our inference based on the case laid out in Part II that establishments will not change of their own accord.

---

[4]"Public Trust in Government 1958–2013 (2013)", Pew *Research Center*, October 18. Retrieved from http://www.people-press.org/2013/10/18/trust-in-government-interactive/. Public trust in 1958 was 73% and has steadily fallen thereafter to 19% in 2013.

[5]It claims to have done so however by conflating support for welfare recipients with assistance to the productive middle class. Mason, Jeff and Felsenthal, Mark (2014), "Obama to offer new tax breaks for workers in election year budget pitch", *Reuters* (March 4). Retrieved from http://finance.yahoo.com/news/obama-offer-tax-breaks-workers-120000753.html.

[6]Boccia, Romina; Fraser, Alison Acosta and Goff, Emily (2013), "Federal Spending by the Numbers: Government Spending Trends in Graphics, Tables, and Key Points", *Heritage Foundation* (August). Retrieved from http://www.heritage.org/research/reports/2013/08/federal-spending-by-the-numbers-2013. "Though deficits will decline for a few more years, existing spending cuts and tax increases will not prevent them from rising soon, and within a decade exceeding $1 trillion once again. Driving this is federal spending which, despite sequestration cuts, will grow 69% by 2023".

Table 16.1.   Chronic budget deficits.

The Federal Budget, 1993–2013

IN BILLIONS OF INFLATION-ADJUSTED 2013 DOLLARS

Fiscal Year	Mandatory Spending	Discretionary Spending	Net Interest	Total Spending	Total Revenue	Surplus/ Deficit
1993	1,011	813	299	2,123	1,739	-384
1994	1,058	799	299	2,156	1,856	-300
1995	1,067	787	335	2,189	1,953	-237
1996	1,115	755	342	2,211	2,059	-152
1997	1,127	761	339	2,228	2,197	-30
1998	1,181	758	331	2,270	2,366	95
1999	1,220	776	312	2,308	2,478	170
2000	1,265	817	296	2,379	2,693	314
2001	1,309	843	268	2,420	2,587	167
2002	1,413	938	218	2,570	2,368	-202
2003	1,481	1,032	192	2,705	2,232	-473
2004	1,512	1,093	196	2,801	2,297	-504
2005	1,561	1,146	218	2,924	2,548	-377
2006	1,615	1,163	259	3,038	2,754	-284
2007	1,611	1,157	263	3,032	2,854	-179
2008	1,732	1,233	274	3,239	2,741	-498
2009	2,244	1,327	200	[3,772]	2,257	-1,515
2010	2,031	1,430	208	3,670	2,296	-1,374
2011	2,106	1,401	239	3,746	2,395	-1,351
2012	2,073	1,313	225	[3,611]	2,501	-1,110
2013*	2,020	1,213	223	3,455	2,813	-642

* Estimate.   ☐ Highest spending level   ☐ First year of Budget Control Act

Source: Office of Management and Budget, *Historical Tables: Budget of the U.S. Government, FY 2014*, Tables 8.1 and 1.1, April 2013, http://www.whitehouse.gov/omb/budget/ Historicals (accessed May 1, 2013); and Congressional Budget Office, *Updated Budget Projections: Fiscal Years 2013 to 2023*, May 2013, Table 1–1, http://www.cbo.gov/publication/44172 (accessed May 15, 2013).

Federal Spending by the Numbers 2013 ☎ heritage.org

Pot and Kettle

Our position can be attacked more convincingly by arguing that the pot is blacker than the kettle; that is, by counterclaiming that small democratic government (the pot) is worse than big pipe dream government (the kettle). This line of defense may concede all the allegations we raise against modern ideocracies, yet still allow big government advocates to assert that switching to "compassionate" democratic free enterprise is a grave mistake because it will strengthen the upper hand of "capitalists", Wall Street, and big business. The small government democratic free enterprise we advocate of course supports the elimination of Wall Street's, and big business's upper hand, but critics can brush our caveats aside by asserting that small governments will be too small to prevent monopolists and oligopolists from increasing their power.

Accordingly, US's and the EU's future without big government from this perspective it can be argued would be worse, not better. If pipe dream government does not hold the line, critics contend, growth retardation will intensify, stagnation will turn into depression, unemployment and underemployment will increase, income and wealth disparities will become astronomical, conditions for Black, Hispanic and European Muslim citizens will become intolerable and global harmony will be destroyed. A similar defense was widely and effectively employed by communists during the cold war to try to persuade people that although Stalin's crimes against humanity were regrettable, the Soviet Union remained the future's greatest hope.[7]

The methodology for determining whether pipe dream big government is the lesser evil or the greater good has two aspects: efficiency and norms.[8] Efficiency depends on rules governing decision makers' choices, and competitiveness. Critics of capitalism have long insisted that that big business misallocates resources, underutilizes capacities, promotes "planned" obsolescence,[9] and miss-rewards factors of production because monopolists and oligopolists subordinate profit-seeking to other goals like maximizing sales.[10] These claims have some validity, but do not settle matters because big government is also inefficient. Big government

---

[7] Rosefielde, Steven (2010), *Red Holocaust*, London: Routledge.

[8] There is also a middle position. It can be claimed that the results of big or small government are the same. Its validity depends both on the comparative efficiency of both regimes and judgments about their normative merit.

[9] Bulow, Jeremy (1986), "An Economic Theory of Planned Obsolescence", *The Quarterly Journal of Economics*, Vol. 101, No. 4, pp. 729–749.

[10] This is a very complex matter. Both government officials and private businessmen operate in bounded rational environments with multiple objective functions. For example, William Baumol has shown that many firms with market power may prefer to maximize sales subject to a minimally acceptable profit, rather than simply profit maximizing. Firms of this sort operate in an "attractor" space that allows them latitude, but still assures positive profits. Governments by contrast do not have to make profits in their service businesses. Consequently their attractor domains are wider and include a broad range of adverse outcomes. See Rosefielde, Steven and Pfouts, Ralph W. (2014), *Inclusive Economic Theory*, Singapore: World Scientific Publishers.

does not even pretend to profit-seek and acts more often than not as a take it or leave it monopolist.

Both systems fall short of their full competitive production potential making it essential to appraise whether one is more inefficient than the other on theoretical and econometric grounds. Assessments of this sort were routine during the Cold War. The evidence overwhelming supported the conclusion that western market systems (pots) outperformed centrally planned rivals (kettles) using production potential as the benchmark,[11] even before taking account of hidden inflation.[12]

---

[11] Bergson, Abram (1968), *Planning and Productivity under Soviet Socialism*, New York NY: Columbia University Press. Bergson, Abram (1971), "Development Under Two Systems: Comparative Productivity Growth Since 1950", *World Politics*, Vol. 23, No. 4, pp. 579–617. Bergson, Abram (1972), "Comparative National Income in the USSR and the United States", in J.D. Daly, ed., *International Comparisons of Prices and Output, Studies in Income and Wealth*, New York NY: National Bureau of Economic Research, Vol. 37, pp. 145–185. Bergson, Abram (1972), "Productivity under Two Systems: USSR versus the West," in Jan Tinbergen, Abram Bergson, Fritz Machlup and Oskar Morgenstern, eds., *Optimal Social Welfare and Productivity: Comparative View*, New York NY: Barnes and Noble. Bergson, Abram (1978), *Productivity and the Social System — The USSR and the West*, Cambridge, MA: Harvard University Press. Bergson, Abram (1978), "Managerial Risks and Rewards in Public Enterprise", *Journal of Comparative Economics*, Vol. 2, No. 3, pp. 211–225. Bergson, Abram (1987), "Comparative Productivity: The USSR, Eastern Europe and the West", *American Economic Review* (June), Vol. 77, No. 3, pp. 342–357. Bergson, Abram (1989), *Planning and Performance in Socialist Economies*, Boston: Unwin Hyman. Bergson, Abram (1991), "The USSR Before the Fall: How Poor and Why?" *Journal of Economic Perspectives*, No. 5, Fall, pp. 29–44. Bergson, Abram (1994), "The Communist Efficiency Gap: Alternative Measures", *Comparative Economic Studies*, Vol. XXXVI, No. 1, Spring, pp. 1–12. Bergson, Abram (1995), "Neoclassical Norms and the Valuation of National Product in the Soviet Union and Its Post-communist Successor States: Comment", *Journal of Comparative Economics*, Vol. 21, No. 3, pp. 390–393. Rosefielde, Steven; Lovell, Knox; Danilin, Vyachaslav and Materov, Ivan (1985), "Measuring and Improving Enterprise Efficiency in the Soviet Union", *Economica*, Vol. 52, No. 206, pp. 225–234. Rosefielde, Steven (1998), "Comparative Production Potential in the USSR and the West: Pre-Transition Assessments, in Rosefielde, ed., *Efficiency and Russia's Economic Recovery Potential to the Year 2000 and Beyond*, Aldershot, London: Ashgate, pp. 101–135. Rosefielde, Steven (2005), "Tea Leaves and Productivity: Bergsonian Norms for Gauging the Soviet Future", *Comparative Economic Studies*, Vol. 47, No. 2, pp. 259–273.

[12] After the Soviet Union collapsed the CIA halved its purchasing power parity estimates in recognition of the fact that it had previously overvalued the characteristics of Soviet goods. See Rosefielde, Steven, ed. (1998), *Efficiency and Russia's Economic Recovery Potential to the Year 2000 and Beyond*, Aldershot, London: Ashgate.

The methodology for normatively appraising the comparative merit of rival economic systems was devised by Abram Bergson in 1938 and refined thereafter.[13] It is a two-step technique. First, analysts construct a social welfare function that computes the utility of the entire population from each individual's consumption, given everyone's ordinal utility function, conditioned by each individual's views about inequity, social justice and a host of similar contextual variables.[14] The exercise generates a set of aggregate utility scores. Second, these utility outcomes are ranked according to the judge's own welfare norms. He or she may prefer any outcome regardless of how individuals view their own utility. For example, misogynists may feel that women's utility is unimportant and chose an economic order that privileges men. Or in keeping with our theme, some judges might rule that even though compassionate democratic free enterprise systems provide vastly superior levels of per capita income, and superior economic growth, they should be shunned in favor of pipe dreams that promise (but have not yet delivered) lower Gini coefficients.[15]

These examples demonstrate that no system can ever be universally acclaimed if people's values vary across broad spectrums. Nonetheless, an informed social consensus can be constructed on broad classes of preferred and dis-preferred systems by using the production potential standard as a benchmark, inventorying the key sub-indicators and debating the normative opportunity costs. Consensus is likely because the production potentials of anti-competitive systems are strikingly inferior in terms of per capita gross domestic product (GDP) and sustained economic growth

---

[13] Bergson, Abram (1938), "A Reformulation of Certain Aspects of Welfare Economics," *Quarterly Journal of Economics*, Vol. 52, No. 1, pp. 310–234. Bergson, Abram (1976), "Social Choice and Welfare Economics under Representative Government", *Journal of Public Economics*, Vol. 6, No. 3, pp. 171–190. Bergson, Abram (1954), "The Concept of Social Welfare", *Quarterly Journal of Economics*, Vol. 68, No. 2, pp. 233–252. Bergson, Abram (1966), *Essays in Normative Economics*, Cambridge, MA: Harvard University Press. Rosefielde, Steven (1981), "Knowledge and Socialism", in Steven Rosefielde, ed., *Economic Welfare and the Economics of Soviet Socialism*, London: Cambridge University Press, pp. 5–24.

[14] Rosefielde, Steven and Pfouts, Ralph W. (2014), *Inclusive Economic Theory*, Singapore: World Scientific Publishers.

[15] China's market communist Gini coefficient may be as much as double Taiwan's market capitalist figure.

(purged of hidden inflation). Two examples should suffice. South Korea's per capita GDP is 18 times higher than North Korea's, even though per capita incomes in both countries were virtually identical in 1947.[16]

Per capita income in Singapore surpasses America by a wide margin and Taiwan is rapidly catching up. Both are competitive small government market driven economies that are not being dragged down by politocracy. Both have Gini coefficients well below America. It should not be difficult to build a social consensus about comparative merit even though some judges may always disagree.

This evidence is consistent with Bergson's assessment. He maintained that if all parties participated in good faith, democracies should be able to find an amicable middle ground.[17] He could not prove it, and neither can we, but it seems if people dispassionately exam the facts, it would be difficult to support a consensus in favor big government ideocracies based on their inferior performance.

Teething Problems

The productivity of new institutions and technologies tend to be low when they are introduced, rising rapidly thereafter along learning or experience curves.[18] Big government is constantly introducing new technologies to manage its programs. Some fail, and others may have long gestation periods. Consequently, it always can be argued that today's economic turmoil does not reflect inherent deficiencies of big government. It is merely a normal aspect of the teething process that will soon give way to better times. Pipe dream advocates according urge the faithful to stay the course. They could be right. But how many times must promises be

---

[16] The figures for 2011 are respectively $31.9 and $1.8 thousand per capita for South and North Korea. See Central Intelligence Agency (CIA), *World Factbook North Korea and South Korea*, 2014. Retrieved from https://www.cia.gov/library/publications/the-world-factbook/geos/ks.html.

[17] Bergson, Abram (1976), "Social Choice and Welfare Economics under Representative Government", *Journal of Public Economics*, Vol. 6, No. 3, pp. 171–190.

[18] Teplitz, Charles, J. (1991), *The Learning Curve Deskbook: A Reference Guide to Theory, Calculations, and Applications*, New York NY: Quorum Books.

broken before one recognizes that the deficiencies of insider big government are endemic; that the system will never outgrow its teething problems?

Yes, big government ideocracies could be lesser evils after they outgrow their teething problems; but the evidence from Brussels, Moscow and Pyongyang is not compelling.

Chapter **17**

Prospects

There are initiatives underway for each of the reforms recommended in the previous chapters. But the initiatives are not coordinated, and due to doublethink the people involved do not recognize that they are linked by a larger need.

The origins of the problems of economic crisis, increasing stagnation and global polarization lie in the political system — they are not primarily economic.[1] Again, we are in a world much like that of the Ancient Regime. A series of finance ministers in the French government of the 18th century tried to restore solvency to the public finances. Their recommended policies were similar — to restore the public credit by cutting spending; to more evenly distribute the burden of taxation; and to end

---

[1] "India Central Bank Chief Warns of Another Market Crash", *Yahoo News!* (August 6, 2014). Retrieved from http://news.yahoo.com/india-central-bank-chief-warns-another-market-crash-190447924--finance.html. "India's central bank governor, renowned for forecasting the 2008 financial meltdown, has warned that the world economy faces risk of another market crash as asset prices surge".

Increasing global financial instability stems from investors chasing ever higher yields, Raghuram Rajan, a former International Monetary Fund (IMF) chief economist, told the Central Banking Journal. "We are back to the 1930s, in a world of 'competitive easing'," Rajan said, referring to ultra-low interest rate policies pursued by the US Federal Reserve, the Bank of Japan and the Bank of England in a bid to stimulate their economies and spur growth.

"Back then, it was competitive devaluation (of currencies), but competitive easing could lead to competitive devaluation", says Rajan.

the special privileges of insiders (the court, the nobility and the church) in regard to both business (monopoly grants) and taxation (exemptions from taxation). In every instance the finance ministers ultimately failed to get their policies pursued. The resistance of the privileged was too great.

We are in a very similar situation today. In China the lock of the Communist Party on the government means that a successful transition to an economy driven by the consumer is unlikely because insiders in government corporations and in public offices are preventing it. In Europe a federal bureaucracy insulated from public opinion pursues its own enrichment. In America moneyed interests and big social advocacy in a close alliance with political parties have virtually complete control of government.

In situations such as these proposals for reform are denounced as unnecessary and pernicious. They are side-lined, never to be implemented.

It follows that the route to avoiding future financial crises and to restoring economic growth is initially a political road, not an economic one. Only if heightened public awareness (consciousness-raising) permits the termination of establishment political control can there be reform. Russian style sovereign democracy has become common. It is not a system of governance which is in the public's interest. Everywhere the sovereign is a class of insiders empowered by money.

Reforming the Political Process

In America the critical first step is to reform the financing of elections.

Until the campaign finance problem is solved, true public servants cannot get elected and those that do get elected owe a significant debt to private interests that expect to be paid back in some form by the politicians they bankroll.

There are many proposals as to how campaign finance reform can be done (some require amendments to the American Constitution, for example; others do not). Several not-for-profit organizations are pursuing reform. It is less important what particular method is adopted than it is that something of significance be done soon. If American politicians are suddenly independent of private financial backers, then legislation and executive leadership that is truly in the public interest will become possible.

Reducing the Size of Government

The second step is to dramatically reduce the size of government, thereby permitting two things to happen:

1. Placing the finances of the nation on a sound basis by ending deficit spending and reducing debt[2] (see Figure 17.1);
2. Improving the effectiveness of public purposes, including defense, economic growth, reduction of poverty, and strengthening of the middle class — that is, of all the purposes promised by insiders and not delivered because of fraud, inefficiency, waste and the continuing advantage to insiders of not resolving the problems.

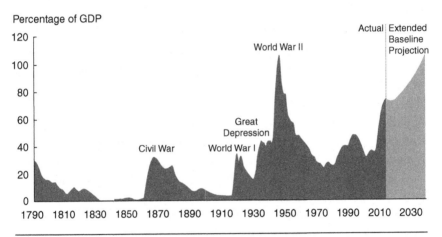

Figure 17.1.   Federal debt held by the public.

---

[2] Stockman, David (2014), "Krugman's Latest Debt Denial: Why His Two Magic Numbers Don't Cut It", (July 23). Retrieved from http://seekingalpha.com/article/2332785-krugmans-latest-debt-denial-why-his-two-magic-numbers-dont-cut-it.

   "Even accepting CBO's 'rosy scenario' outlook (see Figure 17.1), it's not evident that it has declared an end to the debt spiral. In fact, it projects publicly-held treasury debt to soar from $12 trillion today to about $52 trillion by 2039. Most people would judge that a spiral. Indeed, as shown in the CBO graph (Figure 17.1) based on "current policy", the public debt ratio is heading sharply upwards to more than 100% of GDP".

Reducing Regulation of Business

The third step is to get the government out of the protection of business interests by reducing our over-reliance on regulation and embracing reform. Regulation is always presented as pro-consumer, but rarely is, much more commonly granting subsidies or protected markets to business interests. The most important initiative is to completely restructure the banking industry. Restructuring should end the concentration of banking assets into a few enormous banks; return widespread competition to the financial sector; enforce banking regulation in a serious fashion (foregoing fines in preference to penalties against executives); and ending the forays of banks into non-banking sectors of the economy.

Restoring Market Competition to the Global Economy

The fourth step is to restore free competition to the global economy. What is now happening is that government despite its lip-service to competitive markets is permitting the growth of enormous firms and consolidation of industries. Then the government regulates the companies — bureaucratically unless the politicians see an advantage of getting involved; when that happens, government regulation is by the politicians.

Slowly, world markets are being changed from competitive to oligopolistic, and the public pays a substantial price.

Avoiding financial crises and economic stagnation requires governments to cease to permit, even favor, the creation of large firms in increasingly concentrated industries.[3] It also requires government to cease to regulate firms closely so that market forces, essentially the preferences of consumers, dictate price, quality and quantity, rather than regulators.

These two reforms must be made simultaneously. If industries are reformed into a less concentrated, more competitive form with many smaller firms, then current regulation levels must be reduced. To deconcentrate an industry into many smaller firms and leave current levels of government regulation in place will smother the firms with costs and inefficiencies. It may be a result worse than the current situation.

If the current highly concentrated structure of many industries is left intact, then some aspects of current regulation are not inappropriate and

---

[3]"Black Swans and Endogenous Uncertainty", *Forbes,* March 1, 2014. Retrieved from http://www.forbes.com/sites/johnmauldin/2014/03/02/black-swans-and-endogenous-uncertainty/.

should remain. To substantially deregulate the existing large firms is to permit the large firms to engage in anti-consumer behavior without any restraint.

There is a classic example of this latter danger. In the 1990s in America the FED pressed for the deregulation of the nation's banks. Alan Greenspan insisted that market forces would effectively discipline the industry to consumer's benefit. But the industry was highly concentrated and the large firms had substantial political influence. There was no attempt to reduce the size of large firms or to lessen concentration in the industry. Deregulation without lessened concentration allowed large banks to grow rapidly and increase the concentration of the industry further. Protected, even championed, by political interests, the big banks embarked on extensive speculation and poor business practices that resulted in the financial crisis of 2007–2008. If banking was to be dominated by a few large firms, then it should not have been deregulated. If it was to have been deregulated, then banking should have been restructured into a more perfectly competitive market.

There is more that needs to be done, but these four steps will reverse the downward spiral of the world economy into crises, stagnation and repolarization. They will revive the global economic activity; promote economic progress, prosperity and international harmony for the long-term.

Unfortunately, what can be done is unlikely to be what will be done for a very long time.[4] It may take something like a second Pearl Harbor, or German invasion of Poland to shock the global community back into its senses.

---

[4]"IMF cuts global growth outlook, warns of stagnation risk in rich nations", *Reuters,* July 24, 2014. "The IMF warned that only some of the factors leading to the reduction were temporary, and said richer nations in particular faced the risk of economic stagnation unless they do more to boost growth through deeper reforms, such as investing in infrastructure or changing tax laws". http://news.yahoo.com/imf-cuts-global-growth-outlook-warns-stagnation-risk-150310757.html.

Ruchir Sharma, "How Spending Sapped the Global Recovery", *Wall Street Journal,* January 16, 2015. "Before anyone rushes to spend, however, it is worth noting that the big emerging nations — China, Russia and Brazil — have just tried a full-throttle experiment in stimulus spending, and it failed. The average growth rate for emerging economies excluding China has fallen to 2.5% today, from more than 7% at the height of the spending campaign. The growth rate is the lowest in four decades, outside of a global recession. For leaders in these countries, stimulus is now a bad word". http://www.wsj.com/articles/ruchir-sharma-how-spending-sapped-the global-recovery-14213366768.

Conclusion

Global economic liberalization's promise of steadily improving living standards has given way to a very different world order. It is crisis-prone, economically stagnant, and politically fragile. The current generation of political leaders in the developed countries considers the problems serious enough to justify continuous deficit spending and expansionary monetary policy. This has been going on for decades. These "more of the same" anti-austerity measures are not the fundamental responses needed if the dangers of another financial crisis, secular stagnation, depression, burgeoning inequality, middle class alienation, and intensified international turmoil are to be averted. Instead, leaders glibly assure us that eventually there will be clear sailing ahead. Unfortunately, this is wishful thinking.

The origins of the problems of economic crisis, stagnation, inequality, excessive middle class taxation and international polarization lie in the political system and are neither self-correcting nor transitory. The problems do not arise from differences over classical economic theory, or the goal of advancing the public good. They stem from the will to power and wealth of self-styled governing elites and their supporters that trample the democratic rule of constitutional law.

The challenge posed by secular stagnation, crises, decay and discord today cannot be adequately understood in the neoclassical economic terms in which most of us think. The main driver is not ethically motivated Enlightenment reason. It is self-seeking insider globalization: That is, the

179

worldwide quest by national establishments and their allies to maximize rewards for themselves derived from government programs, corruption, self-serving regulation, over-taxation, fiscal leverage, credit expansion, liberalization, supra-nationalization and emergent world government.

Globalization on west's idealistic terms is dead not only because of the establishments' hypocrisy, but because America's and the EU's expedient policies have afforded Russia, China and several middle eastern nations a major opportunity to bend the global power balance their way with multiple instruments including military force, flouting the START arms control agreement, subversion, intimidation, market power and what Vladimir Putin calls "enlightened conservative" authoritarian ideologies. The resulting struggle for hegemony will exacerbate the gathering economic storm.

The world economy and the national economies of which it is composed will, of course, always experience ups and downs, but today's trajectory is ominous. It can be reversed; economic correctives are readily available, but they require political, business and social activist insiders to make unpalatable personal sacrifices for the greater good. This they strongly resist in private while claiming publicly to do the opposite. The route to advancing the public good by avoiding future financial crises, restoring economic growth, mitigating international conflicts therefore lies in preventing politicians from riding roughshod over prudent policies. The past several decades have made it clear that it is pointless to wait for establishments to do the right things themselves.

There are no easy fixes to the increasing turmoil into which the world is falling because the advocacy of the public good by entrenched politicians and government administrators is hypocritical.[1] Miracles should not be

---

[1] "Power Players New book: Being assigned to Hillary Clinton's Secret Service Detail 'a Form of Punishment'", *ABC News* (August 14, 2014). Retrieved from http://news.yahoo. com/blogs/power-players-abc-news/new-book--being-assigned-to-hillary-clinton-s-secret-service-detail-%E2%80%9Ca-form-of-punishment%E2%80%9D-213322171.html. "She is so nasty to agents that being assigned to her detail is considered a form of

expected. Nonetheless, a different and more effective path is available if democratic publics begin to appreciate the present danger. The people can take direct action to reclaim their sovereignty. They can devise strategies for constraining the rapacity of insiders, including those set forward in this book, and clip the wings of their "public servants".

---

punishment", Kessler told "Top Line" of Clinton, who continues to receive Secret Service protection as a former first lady.

It shines a light on her character", Kessler said. "She claims to be a champion of the little people, and she is going to help the middle class. And, in fact, she treats these people around her, [who] would lay down their lives for her like sub-humans; and I think voters need to consider that". Kessler, Ronald (2014), *The First Family Detail*, New York: Random House.

Bibliography

Acemoglu, Daron and Robinson, James. A. (2012), *Why Nations Fail: The Origins of Power, Prosperity and Poverty*, New York NY: Crown.

Acharya, Viral V. *et al.* (eds.) (2011), *Regulating Wall Street: The Dodd–Frank Act and the New Architecture of Global Finance*, New York NY: John Wiley and Sons.

Aron, Raymond (2001), *Opium of the Intellectuals*, Brunswick New Jersey NJ: Transaction.

Barro, Robert J. and Sala-i-Martin, Xavier (1995), *Economic Growth*, New York NY: McGraw-Hill.

Baumol, William (1959), *Business Behavior, Value and Growth*, New York NY: Macmillan.

Bell, Daniel (1976), *The Cultural Contradictions of Capitalism*, New York NY: Basic Books.

Bell, Daniel (2000), *The End of Ideology: On the Exhaustion of Political Ideas in the Fifties*, Cambridge MA: Harvard University Press.

Bergson, Abram (1938), "A Reformulation of Certain Aspects of Welfare Economics," *Quarterly Journal of Economics*, Vol. 52, No. 1, pp. 310–334.

Bergson, Abram (1954), "The Concept of Social Welfare," *Quarterly Journal of Economics*, Vol. 68, No. 2 (May), pp. 233–252.

Bergson, Abram (1966), *Essays in Normative Economics*, Cambridge MA: Harvard University Press.

Bergson, Abram (1968), *Planning and Productivity under Soviet Socialism*, New York NY: Columbia University Press.

Bergson, Abram (1971), "Development under Two Systems: Comparative Productivity Growth Since 1950," *World Politics*, Vol. 23, No. 4, pp. 579–617.

Bergson, Abram (1972a), "Productivity under Two Systems: USSR versus the West," in Jan Tinbergen, Abram Bergson, Fritz Machlup and Oskar Morgenstern, eds., *Optimal Social Welfare and Productivity: Comparative View*, New York NY: Barnes and Noble.

Bergson, Abram (1972b), "Comparative National Income in the USSR and the United States," in J.D. Daly, ed., *International Comparisons of Prices and Output, Studies in*

Income and Wealth, New York NY: National Bureau of Economic Research, Vol. 37, pp. 145–185.

Bergson, Abram (1976), "Social Choice and Welfare Economics under Representative Government," *Journal of Public Economics*, Vol. 6, No. 3, pp. 171–190.

Bergson, Abram (1978), *Productivity and the Social System — The USSR and the West*, Cambridge MA: Harvard University Press.

Bergson, Abram (1987a), "Comparative Productivity: The USSR, Eastern Europe and the West," *American Economic Review*, Vol. 77, No. 3, pp. 342–357.

Bergson, Abram (1987b), "Managerial Risks and Rewards in Public Enterprise," *Journal of Comparative Economics*, Vol. 2, No. 3, pp. 211–225.

Bergson, Abram (1989), *Planning and Performance in Socialist Economies*, Boston: Unwin Hyman.

Bergson, Abram (1991), "The USSR Before the Fall: How Poor and Why?" *Journal of Economic Perspectives*, Vol. 5, No. 4, pp. 29–44.

Bergson, Abram (1994), "The Communist Efficiency Gap: Alternative Measures," *Comparative Economic Studies*, Vol. XXXVI, No. 1, pp. 1–12.

Bergson, Abram (1995), "Neoclassical Norms and the Valuation of National Product in the Soviet Union and Its Post-Communist Successor States: Comment," *Journal of Comparative Economics*, Vol. 21, No. 3, pp. 390–393.

Bhagwati, Jadish (2002), *Free Trade Today*, Princeton NJ: Princeton University Press.

Blanchard, Olivier, J. and Gali, Jordi (2007), "Real Wage Rigidities and the New Keynesian Model," *Journal of Money, Credit, and Banking*, Vol. 39, No. 1, pp. 35–65.

Blaug, Mark (1997), *Economic Theory in Retrospect*, Cambridge: Cambridge University Press, Chapter 2, Section 19, pp. 59–62.

Blokker, Paul (2015), "The European Crisis as a Crisis of Democratic Capitalism," in Steven Rosefielde and Bruno Dallago, *Transformation and Crisis in Russia, Ukraine, Central and Eastern Europe: Challenges and Prospects*, London: Routledge.

Bulow, Jeremy (1986), "An Economic Theory of Planned Obsolescence," *The Quarterly Journal of Economics*, Vol. 101, No. 4, pp. 729–749.

Buss, David (2008), *Evolutionary Psychology: The New Science of the Mind*, Boston: Omegatype.

Calomiris, Charles W. and Haber, Stephen H. (2014), *Fragile by Design: The Political Origins of Banking Crises and Scarce Credit*, Princeton NJ: Princeton University Press.

Campbell, R.H. and Skinner, S.S. (1981), *The Glasgow Edition of the Works and Correspondence of Adam Smith*, Vol. 2a, Indianapolis: Liberty Fund, p. 10.

Christensen, Clayton M. and Bever, Derek van (2014), "The Capitalist's Dilemma," *Harvard Business Review*, June.

Curry, William Sims (2014), *Government Abuse*, New Brunswick NJ: Transaction.

Dahl, Robert (1971), *Polyarchy: Participation and Opposition*, New Haven: Yale University Press.

Denton, Derek (2006), *The Primordial Emotions: The Dawning of Consciousness*, London: Oxford University Press.

Diamond, Douglas and Dybvig, Phillip (1983), "Bank Runs, Deposit Insurance, and Liquidity," *Journal of Political Economy*, Vol. 91, No. 3, pp. 401–419.

Dixon, Peter B. and Jorgenson, Dale W. (2013), *Handbook of Computable General Equilibrium Modeling SET*, Vols. 1A and 1B, Amsterdam: Elsevier.

Dollar, David and Kraay, Aart (2002), "Spreading the Wealth," *Foreign Affairs*, Vol. 81, pp. 120–133.

Dreyfus, Hubert (1990), *Being-in-the-World: A Commentary on Heidegger's Being and Time, Division* I, Cambridge, Massachusetts, & London: MIT Press.

Duménil, Gerard and Lévy, Dominique (2013), *The Crisis of Neoliberalism*, Cambridge MA: Harvard University Press.

Elias, Norbert and Scotson, John (2009), *The Established and the Outsiders*, Dublin: University College.

Feinstein, Charles (1975), *Socialism, Capitalism and Economic Growth: Essays Presented to Maurice Dobb*, Cambridge: Cambridge University Press.

Ferguson, Niall (2008), *The Ascent of Money: A Financial History of the World*, New York NY: Penguin.

Festinger, Leon (1957), *A Theory of Cognitive Dissonance*, Stanford: Stanford University Press.

Fisher, Irving (1930), *The Theory of Interest*, Clifton NJ: Augustus M. Kelley.

Fox, Elaine (2008), *Emotion Science: An Integration of Cognitive and Neuroscientific Approaches*, New York NY: Palgrave MacMillan.

Freeman, Jody and Minow, Martha, eds. (2009), *Government by Contracting: Outsourcing and Democracy*, Cambridge MA: Harvard University Press.

Freud, Sigmund Shlomo (1923), *Beyond the Pleasure Principle*.

Freud, Sigmund Shlomo (1927), *The Ego and the Id*, (*Das Ich und das Es*).

Freud, Sigmund Shlomo (1930), *Civilization and its Discontents*, [Das Unbehagen in der Kultur ("The Uneasiness in Culture")].

Fromm, Eric (1992), *The Revision of Psychoanalysis*, Colorado: Westview Press.

Fukuyama, Francis (2006), *The End of History and the Last Man Standing*, New York NY: Free Press.

Fukuyama, Francis (2014), "America in Decay: The Sources of Political Dysfunction," *Foreign Affairs*, September/October.

Gadamer, Hans-Georg (2004), *Truth and Method*, (2nd rev. edn.), trans. by J. Weinsheimer and D.G. Marshall, New York NY: Crossroad.

Geithner, Timothy F. (2014), *Stress Test*, New York NY: Crown.

Giddens, Anthony (1998), *The Third Way: The Renewal of Social Democracy*, London: Polity.

Giddens, Anthony (2000), *The Third Way and its Critics*, London: Polity.

Grauwe, Paul De (2010), "Top-Down versus Bottom-Up Macroeconomics," *CESifo Economic Studies*, Vol. 56, No. 4, pp. 465–497.

Green, Donald and Higgins, Christopher (1997), *SOVMOD I: A Macroeconomic Model of the Soviet Union*, New York NY: Academic Press, Harcourt Brace and Jovanovich.

Greenspan, Alan (2013), "Never Saw it Coming," *Foreign Affairs*, November/December.

Gudrais, Elizabeth (2014), "Disrupted Lives: Sociologist Matthew Desmond Details the Devastating Effects of Eviction on America's Poor," *Harvard Magazine*, Vol. 116, pp. 38–43.

Haberler, Gottfried von (1976), "The Monetary Approach to the Balance of Payments," *Journal of Economic Literature*, Vol. 14, No. 4, pp. 1324–1328.

Hartmann, Thom (2013), *The Crash of 2016: The Plot to Destroy America — And What We Can Do to Stop It*, New York NY: Twelve.

Hegel, Georg Wilhelm Friedrich (2001), *The Philosophy of History*, Kitchener, Ontario, Canada: Batoche.

Heller, Walter (1966), *New Dimensions of Political Economy*, Cambridge MA: Harvard University Press.

Hobbes, Thomas (1651), *Leviathan or the Matter, Forme and Power of a Common Wealth Ecclesiasticall and Civil.*

Hoeller, Peter; Joumard, Isabelle and Isabell Koske (2014), "Reducing Income Inequality While Boosting Economic Growth: Can it be Done? Evidence from OECD Countries," *The Singapore Economic Review*, Vol. 59, No. 1, pp. 1–22.

Hoffer, Eric (2002), *The True Believer: Thoughts on the Nature of Mass Movements*, New York NY: Harper Perennial Modern Classics.

Horáková, Martina and Jordan, Amy (2014), *Directory of Financial Regulators 2014*, London: Central Banking Books.

Jacoby, Russell (2000), *The End of Utopia: Politics and Culture in an Age of Apathy*, New York NY: Basic Books.

Johnson, Simon (1957), *Models of Man*, New York NY: Wiley.

Johnson, Simon and Kwak, James (2012), 13 *Bankers: Wall Street Takeover and the Next Financial Meltdown*, New York NY: Vintage.

Johnson, Simon and Kwak, James (2013), *White House Burning: Our National Debt and What it Means to You*, New York NY: Vintage.

Jones, Daniel Stedman (2013), *Masters of the Universe: Hayek, Friedman and the Birth of Neoliberal Politics*, Princeton NJ: Princeton University Press.

Kahneman, Daniel (2011), *Thinking, Fast and Slow*, New York NY: Macmillan.

Keynes, John Maynard (1936), *The General Theory of Employment, Interest and Money*, London: Macmillan, Cambridge University Press.

Korhonen, Iikka; Fidrmuc, Jarko and Batorova, Ivana (2012), "Business-Cycle Decoupling," in Steven Rosefielde, Masaaki Kuboniwa and Satoshi Mizobata, eds., *Two Asias: The Emerging Postcrisis Divide*, Singapore: World Scientific, pp. 345–358.

Krugman, Paul (1994), "Competitiveness: A Dangerous Obsession," *Foreign Affairs*, March/April, pp. 28–44.

Krugman, Paul (2009), *The Return of Depression Economics and the Crisis of 2008*, New York NY: WW Norton Company.

Kuhn, Thomas (1996), *The Structure of Scientific Revolutions*, Chicago: University of Chicago Press.

Kydland, Phil and Prescott, Edward (1982), "Time to Build and Aggregate Fluctuations," *Econometrica*, Vol. 50, No. 6, pp. 1345–1370.

Leightner, Jonathan (2014), *The Limits of Monetary, Fiscal, and Trade Policies: International Comparisons and a Solution*, Singapore: World Scientific.

Lipset, Seymore (1983), *Political Man: The Social Bases of Politics*, London: Heinemann.

Locke, John (1689), *An Essay Concerning the True Original Extent and End of Civil Government*.

Lucas, Robert Jr. (1972), "Expectations and the Neutrality of Money," *Journal of Economic Theory*, Vol. 4, No. 2, pp. 103–124.

Macmillan, Harold (1939), *The Middle Way: A Study of the Problem of Economic and Social Progress in a Free and Democratic Society*, London: Macmillan.

Maddison, Angus (2003), *The World Economy: Historical Statistics*, Paris: OECD.

Magee, Bryan (1997), *The Philosophy of Schopenhauer*, Oxford: Oxford University Press.

Maki, Dennis and Spindler, Zane (1975), "The Effect of Unemployment Compensation on the Rate of Unemployment in Great Britain," *Oxford Economic Papers*, New Series, Vol. 27, No. 3, pp. 440–454.

Malia, Martin (1994), *The Soviet Tragedy: A History of Socialism in Russia, 1917–1991*, New York NY: Free Press.

Mankiw, Gregory and Reis, Ricardo (2002), "Sticky Information Versus Sticky Prices: A Proposal To Replace The New Keynesian Phillips Curve," *Quarterly Journal of Economics*, Vol. 117, No. 4, pp. 1295–1328.

Marglin, Stephen (2008), *The Dismal Science: How Thinking like an Economists Undermines Community*, Cambridge MA: Harvard University Press.

McCloskey, Donald (1993), "Review of Alexander Rosenberg, Mathematic Politics or Science of Diminishing Returns," *The History of Science Society*, Vol. 84, No. 4, pp. 838–839.

Mian, Atif and Amir Sufi (2014), *House of Debt*, Chicago: University of Chicago Press.

Mills, Quinn and Rosefielde, Steven (2009), *Rising Nations: What America Should Do*, New York NY: Amazon.

Neuberger, Egon (1966), "Libermanism, Computopia, and Visible Hand: The Question of Informational Efficiency," *American Economic Review*, Vol. 56, Nos. 1/2, March, pp. 131–144.

Obstfeld, Maurice (2001), "International Macroeconomics: Beyond the Mundell–Fleming Model," *IMF Staff Papers*, Vol. 47.

Orwell, George (1945), *Animal Farm*, London: Secker and Warburg.

Orwell, George (1949), *Nineteen Eighty Four*, London: Secker and Warburg.

Piattoni, Simona (forthcoming), "Institutional Innovations and EU Legitimacy after the Crisis," in Steven Rosefielde and Bruno Dallago, *Transformation and Crisis in Russia, Ukraine, Central and Eastern Europe: Challenges and Prospects*, London: Routledge.

Piketty, Thomas (2014), *Capital in the Twenty-First Century*, Cambridge MA: Harvard University Press.

Plant, Raymond (2009), *The Neo-Liberal State*, Oxford: Oxford University Press.

Popper, Karl (1934), *The Logic of Scientific Discovery*, London: Routledge.

Porter, Michael (1990), *The Competitive Advantage of Nations*, London: Macmillan.

Prasad, Monica (2006), *The Politics of Free Markets: The Rise of Neoliberal Economic Policies in Britain, France, Germany and the United States*, Chicago: University of Chicago Press.

Rauniyar, Ganesh and Kanbur, Ravi (2010), "Inclusive Development: Two Papers on Conceptualization, Application and the ADB Perspective," *Journal of the Asia Pacific Economy*, Vol. 15, No. 4, pp. 437–469.

Reinhart, Carmen and Rogoff, Kenneth (2009), *This Time Will be Different: Eight Centuries of Financial Folly*, Princeton NJ: Princeton University Press.

Reinhart, Carmen; Rogoff, Kenneth and Vincent, Reinhart (2012), "Public Debt Overhangs: Advanced-Economy Episodes since 1800," *Journal of Economic Perspectives*, Vol. 25, No. 3, pp. 69–86.

Rickards, James (2014), *The Death of Money: The Coming Collapse of the International Monetary System*, New York NY: Portfolio Hardcover.

Romer, David (2011), "Endogenous Growth," in *Advanced Macroeconomics* (4th ed.), New York NY: McGraw-Hill, pp.101–149.

Rosefielde, Steven (1981), "Knowledge and Socialism," in Rosefielde, ed., *Economic Welfare and the Economics of Soviet Socialism*, London: Cambridge University Press, pp. 5–24.

Rosefielde, Steven (1982), *False Science: Underestimating the Soviet Arms Buildup*, New Brunswick NJ: Transaction.

Rosefielde, Steven (1998), "Comparative Production Potential in the USSR and the West: Pre-Transition Assessments, in Rosefielde, ed., *Efficiency and Russia's Economic Recovery Potential to the Year 2000 and Beyond*, Aldershot, London: Ashgate, pp. 101–135.

Rosefielde, Steven (2005a), *Russia in the 21st Century: Prodigal Superpower*, Cambridge: Cambridge University Press.

Rosefielde, Steven (2005b), "Tea Leaves and Productivity: Bergsonian Norms for Gauging the Soviet Future," *Comparative Economic Studies*, Vol. 47, No. 2, pp. 259–273.

Rosefielde, Steven (2007), *Russian Economy from Lenin to Putin*, New York NY: Wiley.

Rosefielde, Steven (2010), *Red Holocaust*, London: Routledge.

Rosefielde, Steven (2012), "Economics of the Military-Industrial Complex," in Michael Alexeev and Shlomo Weber, eds., *The Oxford Handbook of Russian Economy*, Oxford: Oxford University Press.

Rosefielde, Steven (2013a), "Russian Economic Reform 2012: "Déjà vu All Over Again," in Stephen Blank, ed., *Politics and Economics in Putin's Russia*, Carlisle Barracks: Strategic Studies Institute and US Army War College.

Rosefielde, Steven (2013b), "Soviet Economy: An Ideocratic Reassessment," *Ekonomicheskaya Nauka Sovremennoy Rossii*, #3.

Rosefielde, Steven (2013c), *Asian Economic Systems*, Singapore: World Scientific.

Rosefielde, Steven (2015), *The Kremlin Strikes Back: Russia and the West after Crimea's Annexation*, Cambridge: Cambridge University Press.

Rosefielde, Steven and Dallago, Bruno (forthcoming), *Transformation and Crisis in Russia, Ukraine, Central and Eastern Europe: Challenges and Prospects*, London: Routledge.

Rosefielde, Steven, Kuboniwa, Masaaki and Mizobata Satoshi (2012), *Two Asias: The Growing Postcrises Divide*, Singapore: World Scientific.

Rosefielde, Steven, Lovell, Knox; Danilin, Vyachaslav and Materov, Ivan (1985), "Measuring and Improving Enterprise Efficiency in the Soviet Union," *Economica*, Vol. 52, No. 206, pp. 225–234.

Rosefielde, Steven and Mills, Quinn (2012), "Global Default" in Steven Rosefielde, Masaaki Kuboniwa and Satoshi Mizobata, eds., *Prevention and Crisis Management: Lessons for Asia from the 2008 Crisis*, Singapore: World Scientific.

Rosefielde, Steven and Mills, Quinn (2013), *Democracy and its Elected Enemies*, Cambridge: Cambridge University Press.

Rosefielde, Steven and Pfouts, Ralph W. (2014), *Inclusive Economic Theory*, Singapore: World Scientific.

Rosefielde, Steven and Razin, Assaf (2012), "The 2008–2009 Global Crisis," in Steven Rosefielde, Masaaki Kuboniwa and Mizobata, Satoshi, eds., *Prevention and Crisis Management: Lessons for Asia from the 2008 Crisis*, Singapore: World Scientific.

Rosenberg, Alexander (1994), *Mathematic Politics or Science of Diminishing Returns*, Chicago: University of Chicago Press.

Rosenberg, Alex and Curtain, Tyler (2013), "What is Economics Good for?" *New York Times*, August 24, 2013. Available at http://opinionator.blogs.nytimes.com/2013/08/24/what-is-economics-good-for/?_r=1.

Rosencranz, Charles (2010), "Bigger is Better: The Case for a Transpacific Economic Union," *Foreign Affairs*, Vol. 89, No. 3, pp. 42–51.

Rousseau, Jean-Jacques (1754), *Discourse on the Origin and Basis of Inequality among Men*, (Discours sur l'origine et les fondements de l'inégalité parmi les hommes).

Samuelson, Paul (1947), *Foundations of Economic Analysis*, Cambridge: Harvard University Press.

Sartre, Jean-Paul (2001), *Being and Nothingness: An Essay in Phenomenological Ontology*, New York NY: Citadel Press.

Schmitt, Carl (2004), *Legality and Legitimacy*, Durham NC: Duke University Press.

Schopenhauer, Arthur (2010), *The World as Will and Representation*, Vol. 1, Cambridge: Cambridge University Press.

Selten, Reinhard (2002), "What is Bounded Rationality?," in Gerd Gigerenzer, and Reinhard Selten, eds., *Bounded Rationality The Adaptive Toolbox*, Cambridge MA: MIT Press.

Sen, Amartya (2010), *The Idea of Justice*, London: Penguin.

Sen, Amartya (2013), "Personal Utilities and Public Judgments: Or What's Wrong with Welfare Economics," *Economic Journal*, Vol. 89, No. 3, pp. 537–588.

Shiller, Garry (2005), *Irrational Exuberance*, Princeton NJ: Princeton University Press.

Simon, Herbert, Egidi, Massimo, Marris, Robin and Viale, Riccardo (1992), *Economics, Bounded Rationality and the Cognitive Revolution*, Aldershot, London: Ashgate.

Simon, Herbert (1955), "A Behavioral Model of Rational Choice," *Quarterly Journal of Economics*, Vol. 59, pp. 99–118.

Simon, Herbert (1982), *Models of Bounded Rationality*, Cambridge MA: Harvard University Press.

Smith, Adam (1776), *Inquiry into the Nature and Causes of the Wealth of Nations*, London: W. Strahan and T. Cadell.

Stiglitz, Joseph (2002), *Globalization and its Discontents*, London: Penguin.

Taylor, John (2009), *Getting Off Track: How Government Actions and Interventional Caused, Prolonged, and Worsened the Financial Crisis*, Palo Alto: Hoover Institution Press.

Thompson, Derek (2014), "How America Pays Taxes — in 10 Not-Entirely-Depressing Charts," *The Atlantic* (April 16). Available at http://www.theatlantic.com/business/archive/2014/04/how-america-pays-taxes-in-10-not-entirely-depressing-charts/360647/.

Thurow, Lester (1980), *Zero Sum Society*, New York NY: Basic Books.

Tucker, Robert (1956), "The Cunning of Reason in Hegel and Marx," *The Review of Politics*, Vol. 18, No. 3, pp. 269–295.

Vanek, Jaroslav (1970), *The General Theory of Labor-Managed Market Economies*, Ithaca NY: Cornell University Press.

Vanek, Jaroslav (1971), *The Participatory Economy. An Evolutionary Hypothesis and a Strategy for Development*, Ithaca NY: Cornell University Press, Vol. 52, No. 1, pp. 310–334.

Vogl, Josef (2014), *The Specter of Capital*, Stanford: Stanford University Press.

Weber, Max (1978), *Economy and Society*, Berkeley CA: University of California Press.

Williamson, John (1993), "Development and the 'Washington Consensus,'" *World Development*, Vol. 21, pp. 1239–1336.

Zucman, Gabriel (2013), "The Missing Wealth of Nations: Are Europe and the U.S. Net Debtors or Net Creditors?" *Quarterly Journal of Economics*, Vol. 128, No. 3, pp. 1321–1364.

Index

Thurow, Lester, 14n6
too big to fail (TBTF), 109, 111n7, 112
Transatlantic Economic Council (TEC), 79, 79n25
transformation, 70, 70n2
transnational entities, politicians supporting, 79–80
Trans Pacific Trade Partnership, 79
2008 financial crisis, 6, 91, 139
    causes of, 100, 107–108, 112–114, 117, 120–122, 124–125
    New Keynesian position and, 81–82
    reform following, 11, 118–119
    stagnation following, 13–29
    V-shaped recovery and, 3–4

Ukraine, 162
UNC Center for Slavic, Eurasian and East European Studies, 44n25
under-consumption, 32, 32n29
underemployment, 22
unemployment
    Affordable Care Act and, 62n12
    BLS and, 129n2
    high, 13–18, 14n7, 15n8, 22, 24n12
    long-term, 155
    maximum number of weeks of, 32n28
    missing workers and, 17
    in US, 13–18, 14n7, 15n8, 17, 22, 24n12, 32n28, 62n12, 129n2, 155
United States (US)
    abusive government of, 14n5, 32, 165
    campaign finance reform in, 174

chronic budget deficits in, 165–166, 165n6
contracting by, 54n47, 73n12
core problems facing, 163
deficit spending in, 155–156, 161, 175
depressed economy in, 8n16, 92n1
east–west polarization and, 87–89, 88n3
entitlements in, 141–142
federal debt, public holding, 175, 175n2
freedom in, 92n1
Gini coefficient of, 170
globalization and, 75, 79–80, 180
infrastructure spending in, 71n5
liberalization in, 75, 79–80, 82–83, 83n31
lost war on poverty in, 34, 34n36, 48n35, 98–101, 105
macroeconomic miasma in, 127
national income accounts, 128
in 1990s, 70
pipe dream big government in, 167
prospects of, 174
sound money in, 160–161
unemployment in, 13–18, 14n7, 15n8, 17, 22, 24n12, 32n28, 62n12, 129n2, 155
urbanization, 104
US. *See* United States
utility, 151–152, 169
utopia, 143n5

Vietnam, 70–72
Volker Rule, 113, 116
Voltaire, 58n3, 146
V-shaped recovery, 3–4